Where Are We Heading?
– Heaven or Hell?

ANDREW BAGULEY

LIGHTHOUSE
PUBLISHING

ISBN 978-1-908483-0-2

Front cover images:
Stairway to heaven: Chinabbud encyclopaedia
Creative Commons License
Lake of Fire (lava flow)
Globe
Front cover design: Julianne Thompson

Typeset by Angela Selfe
Printed and bound in the UK

What do they say about the book?

"I consider Andrew's book to be a worthy contribution to the present religious debate and Christian witness around the subject of eschatology. The discussion of the *eschaton* is rare in many Church circles today and therefore the 'blessed hope' of Christ's return is not front and central, as it was in the New Testament church. It cannot be a coincidence that an eternal perspective on matters pertaining to prophecy and current world events is therefore also missing in public debate. The old adage that 'once we lose sight of Hell, we lose sight of Heaven' is self-evident in theological discourse in the UK church and this timely challenge to ask, 'Where are we heading? Heaven or Hell?' is very much needed and it is to be welcomed".

Danny Stupple
Lay Chair of Eastleigh Synod
Chair of Churches Together in Eastleigh

"Andrew, I have to confess to you that I do hold a somewhat differing view concerning the Lord's coming as I am more a Historist than a Futurist. That is ONLY a personal view and am wide open to being convinced otherwise. I have never allowed that view to prevent me from learning other views. I can happily stand up and say a loud AMEN to all I read in your excellent teaching in this book. I will want to carry copies and encourage people to read it as a needed balanced and readable account of a vital; end-time doctrine"

Rev Dr Tony Stone
Team Support Ministry

CONTENTS

PREFACE

The great evangelist D L Moody wrote this about heaven.

"This book, upon a subject that is very dear to me, is sent forth in the hope that it may give comfort and edification to many; that the weak may be strengthened, the sorrowing consoled, and the despondent encouraged to look with increasing faith to that fairest of fair cities in the Better Land, which is the home of the Redeemer and the redeemed."

A leading divine has recently said:

"When I was a boy I thought of Heaven as a great shining city, with vast walls and domes and spires, and with nobody in it except white angels, who were strangers to me. By and by my little brother died, and I thought of a great city with walls and domes and spires, and a flock of cold, unknown angels, and one little fellow that I was acquainted with. He was the only one that I knew in that country. Then another brother died, and there were two that I knew. Then my acquaintances began to die, and the number continually grew. But it was not until I had sent one of my little children back to GOD, that I began to think I had a little interest there myself. A second, a third, a fourth went, and by that time I had so many acquaintances in Heaven that I did not see any more walls and domes and spires.

I began to think of the residents of the Celestial City. And now so many of my acquaintances have gone there, that it sometimes seems to me that I know more in Heaven than I do on earth."
May the thought of loved ones gone before give additional joy to us as we follow in the way."

Having lost my parents, a niece, a teenage son and my first wife to death, I would also agree with D L Moody's final comment. More and more it seems to me, in this Post-Christian culture, the question arises in people minds, 'What happens after we die?'. The Christian hopefully will answer it by solidly affirming the faith of the Church that heaven is our destination and our home for eternity. Having said that the variety of views, understandings and hopes of Christians about death, heaven, hell, eternal life and the Second coming of Jesus means that there is little unity in the Body of Christ over this issue of our destination when we die. I hope that this contribution will help many, as writing it has also helped me, to crystalize understanding by faith in the Holy Scriptures and the saving work of Jesus Christ upon the Cross.

In writing this book I am hoping that I have to a large extent answered the question raised in my last book "Where are We Heading? Heaven only Knows!"

Andrew Baguley
Devon December 2018

8

INTRODUCTION

As I write this introduction I am struggling with the incessant deluge of bad news, fake news and politically biased news. I am angrier with the deception and disinformation from Government and the way in which the Nation has been treated concerning the Brexit negotiations with the EU. It is so hard to see much truth in anything these days and, certainly, we are lacking in moral and ethical leadership. As a result, I find myself trying to sieve all that is going on through the lens of Scripture. I admire those Christian leaders who can plot a way through the morass of contrary opinions, YouTube video claims, changing church doctrines and conspiracy theories and see the true picture which fits perfectly within scripture. Christian leaders whose stance for truth and prophetic warnings have inspired me are David E Gardner, Wale Babatunde, Tony Pearce, David Hathaway and Clifford Hill. David Gardner preached, taught and wrote over twenty years warning both the Church and the Government of the judgement of God upon the United Kingdom because of sin and disobedience. Wale Babatunde wrote at the turn of the millennium a powerful prophetic word "Great Britain has Fallen!" **(i).** I have to say that very few Christians and fewer politicians have heeded the warnings. If anything, the situation had become worse because of the spiritual blindness and deafness of our multi-faith, anti-Semitic and post Christian society. The same cannot be said of the others who I have named.

Roger French is another Christian leader who inspires me. His Biblical stance for truth has resulted in large attendances at his Bible teaching and at conferences. He wrote much of our jointly authored book "God's Glorious Promise" **(ii).** Dennis

Greenidge is another Christian leader who carries himself, and the gospel, with dignity, authority and humility.

It is very clear to me that neither politicians or scientists have any answers to the judgements of God, natural signs, spiritual signs and wars that shape our everyday lives in this country (nor could they unless they were 'born-again' Christians). It is only through the Holy Spirit that people can discern and know the truth.

In my own prophetic book "Shaken" **(iii)** and my follow-up book "Where are we heading? Heaven only knows!" **(iv)** I too have laid before both Church and State the truth of why we are where we are and what is needed to change the course of Nations' fortunes. Whilst both my books have been well received within evangelical Christian circles as have the many conferences at which Roger French and I have spoken. I am really dismayed at the dis-interest shown by most Christians in these important topics. There is such a lack of knowledge of Scripture and a reluctance to believe it. I am not only talking about the reasons for the political, economic, social and climatic issues before us, but about basic issues of faith and doctrine. False prophets abound in both Church and State. Take, for example, the headlines in the Daily Telegraph in an article by Sarah Knapton (Science Editor) **"There is no God or afterlife".** This statement was taken from the late professor Stephen Hawking's last book published on 16th October 2018 "Brief Answers to Big Questions" **(v).** Professor Hawking is said to have commented that *'No one created the Universe, and no one directs our fate. This, he said, leads me to a profound realisation: there is probably no heaven and after life either. I think belief in the after- life is just wishful thinking'.*

Great Britain has, over many years, fallen into iniquity and incurred God's judgement. The sin and unrighteousness have continued despite warnings and signs from God. The Apostle John in his first letter to the Church brings God's promise to forgive all who will truly repent of their sins and to restore them into relationship with Him. In 1 John 1:9-10 we read *"If we confess our sins, he is faithful and just and will forgive us our sins and purify us from all unrighteousness. If we claim we have not sinned, we make him out to be a liar and his word is not in us."* (1 John 1:9-10).

The New Testament makes it clear that when there is continued disobedience, sin and unrighteousness then God will give both individuals and countries over to the sinful desires of their hearts. Thus we need to take notice of the very clear warnings given to the early church by St Paul in Romans 1:18 – 32: *"The wrath of God is being revealed from heaven against all the godlessness and wickedness of people, who suppress the truth by their wickedness, since what may be known about God is plain to them, because God has made it plain to them. For since the creation of the world God's invisible qualities – his eternal power and divine nature – have been clearly seen, being understood from what has been made, so that people are without excuse. For although they knew God, they neither glorified him as God nor gave thanks to him, but their thinking became futile and their foolish hearts were darkened. Although they claimed to be wise, they became fools and exchanged the glory of the immortal God for images made to look like a mortal human being and birds and animals and reptiles. Therefore, God gave them over in the sinful desires of their hearts to sexual impurity for the degrading of their bodies with one another. They exchanged the truth about God for a lie and worshipped and served created things rather than the Creator – who is forever praised. Amen. Because of this, God gave them over to shameful lusts. Even their women exchanged natural sexual relations for unnatural ones. In the same way the men also abandoned natural relations with women and were inflamed with lust for one another. Men committed shameful acts with other men and received in themselves the due penalty for their error. Furthermore, just as they did not think it worthwhile to retain the knowledge of God, so God gave them over to a depraved mind, so that they do what ought not to be done. They have become filled with every kind of wickedness, evil, greed and depravity. They are full of envy, murder, strife, deceit and malice. They are gossips, slanderers, God-haters, insolent, arrogant and boastful; they invent ways of doing evil; they disobey their parents; they have no understanding, no fidelity, no love, no mercy. Although they know God's righteous decree that those who do such things deserve death, they not only continue to do these very things but also approve of those who practice them".*

We might rightly summarise the current situation of our country and the Church by drawing attention to these four things.

1. we have forsaken God our first love (Revelation 2:4)

2. we are now living without God and his Word (Luke 10:16 and John 3:36)

3. over the past fifteen years we have passed new laws (over twenty) reversing God's laws and promoting sin, unrighteousness and self. For details see my book "Where are We Heading? Heaven only knows!" **(iv)**

4. we have become a country with blood on our hands, not just through recent middle east wars but by abortion and home-grown terrorism, violence and criminal acts, and turning a blind eye to sin (James 4:17).

I rejoice that on Wednesday 10th October 2018 five judges of the Supreme Court unanimously rejected all claims made against the Ashers' Baking Company. This was a wonderful answer to prayer and a victory for gospel freedom. The four-and-a-half-year ordeal for the McArthur family is finally over and they can begin to rebuild both their lives and their business. We pray that God will abundantly prosper them. Unfortunately, their case is another example of the LGBT lobby trying to use new laws to stifle Christian belief and free speech. There are others who have not been successful in defending their actions in the face of LGBT provocation and whose lives and businesses have been adversely affected as a result. There now seems to be NO fear of the Lord in the land. Our Christian heritage and laws that have formed the bedrock of society over hundreds of years are now being eroded away as, each year, new anti-Christ laws are passed releasing a tide of immorality, indecency and sin so great that it would seem as if the Lord has removed His protection from the country unless and until there is a genuine repentance and turning back to God through faith in Jesus Christ as Lord and Saviour. Scoffers and unrepentant sinners will laugh and say "Why would God do this to us?" And we would reply to them and say, "because we have forsaken the Lord God of our Fathers and He has brought all this upon us". This is my paraphrase of 2 Chronicles 7:21-22 that says *"This temple will become a heap of rubble. All who pass by will be appalled and say, 'Why has the LORD done such a thing to this land and to this temple?' People will answer, 'Because they have forsaken the LORD, the God of their ancestors, who brought them out of Egypt, and have embraced other gods, worshipping and serving them-that is why he brought all this disaster on them.'"* Earlier in the same chapter Solomon hears the answer from God *"if my people, who are called by my name, will humble themselves and pray and seek my face and turn from their wicked ways, then I will hear from heaven, and I will forgive their sin and will heal their land. Now my eyes will be open and my ears attentive to the prayers offered in this place. I have chosen and consecrated this temple so that my Name may be there forever. My eyes and my heart will always be there"*. (2 Chronicles 7:14).

God's plan for which Jesus died in our place, was for a new temple to be built of believing, Spirit-filled Christians, who would do all that Jesus did and even greater things, and who, furthermore, would provoke the Jews to jealousy so that they too would repent and turn back to God, thus together following the Final Judgement (Revelation 20) would become a spiritual temple in which for eternity, the Lord would dwell. In other words, God intended through Christ's saving work on the cross to prepare all his people for heaven.

I feel a great sadness in my spirit as I say that I genuinely believe that unbelievers in this nation have almost thrown away their chance of salvation and healing because of continued disobedience to God. This means that hell and not heaven is on the horizon for all who do not believe in the Lord Jesus Christ. (Matthew 5:20 & 2 Peter 2:4). This is the word of the Lord. It is truth. Forget the ungodly laws, policies, pressure groups, self-interest groups, media groups like the BBC and Channel 4, which seek to mislead the nation into believing a lie instead of the truth. They have much to answer for in the Final Judgement that all unbelievers will face. In the mean time you, dear reader, whether you are a Christian or not, can change your destiny. Jesus summed it up like this *"Repent and believe for the kingdom is at hand"* (Mark 1:15). This is vital and urgent. There is no time to prevaricate or make excuses or look at other people or worry about your family and friends. Do it now! After death it is too late –*"Just as people are destined to die once, and after that to face judgement"*. (Hebrews 9:27).

Perhaps our society is now so deceived by current philosophies, Islam and the anti-Christ agenda of the EU and the UK Government that they might, with Blaise Pascal (1623-1663) be saying "I would prefer an intelligent hell to a stupid paradise!"

The reason there is such iniquity and unbelief in our nation and the EU is because there is no fear of God. In fact, the reverse is the case. God is mocked through our legalising, murder, homosexuality, divorce, gay marriage (so-called), gender re-assignment, gambling, drugs, drink and the list goes on. Talk about sticking our tongue out at God or making obscene gestures at Him! God will not be mocked *"Do not be deceived: God cannot be mocked. A man reaps what he sows."* (Galatians 6:7)

What do we choose then, heaven or hell? This book attempts to set out the Biblical truth about these two realities in the prayerful hope that the reader may communicate to non-believers the seriousness of the situation. There is, however, a problem. It is not a problem for God but is for us. Many people, Christians included, do not believe in a literal heaven or hell. Some believe that there are two such places but that they are not physical realities but simply relational experiences. Other people are persuaded by scientists, cosmologists and astrophysicists, and philosophers that there is no such thing. I hope that this book will clearly demonstrate that they are all wrong and that God will forgive them for blocking the way to heaven for millions.

In a Daily Telegraph article about Archbishop of Canterbury on the EU, Christopher Hope, Chief Political Correspondent wrote on 5 June 2018 "The European Union is *"the greatest dream realised for human beings"* for the past 1,500 years, the Archbishop of Canterbury has said. The Archbishop said the EU ranked as the greatest achievement *"since the fall of the western Roman Empire"* in the fifth century. A former Brexit minister said he was "astounded" by the remarks, adding that they showed that the Anglican church was "out of touch" with how people think. I think that Christopher Hope should have added "and the facts, the reality and the demonic evil of the EU Vision make the Archbishop's remarks even more crass and theologically wrong." The leadership of the Church of England, it would now seem, is totally under the control of the Liberal Left Elite in the UK and their political masters in the Illuminati and the Bilderbergers.

The Right Reverend Gavin Ashenden, formerly the Queens Chaplain, replied in Telegraph News on 6th June to the Archbishops statement. He commented that it was a masterful understatement of the error of judgement that Justin Welby has made embracing EU utopianism. He wrote *"There is a convention that clergy don't speak out on political matters where their "flock" or constituency reflect both sides of the argument. It's a sensible one and has saved many an Archbishop from unnecessary humiliation and risking national disrespect. Although those who lean to the Left find the temptation too hard to overcome sometimes, ignoring this convention suggests one of three things: that you think you have a hot-line to God (not impossible but unlikely); that you believe your own personal political judgment is beyond criticism; or that you seriously disrespect your political opponents and their views."* Gavin Ashenden kindly suggested that the jury is currently out! Unfortunately for the Archbishop, the Judge (God) will make that decision very shortly.

It seems that thoughts about the future figure no more important than the next Big Mac meal or the football World Cup! Most people, especially young people, are not helped by Media/Facebook/Twitter and the instant 'news' (false or fake news) that guides the thinking of so many today nor indeed the deliberate distortion of news by Russia and China who are actively involved in spreading disinformation about life, truth, love and hope in both politics, global finance and wars. If you want more facts about Russia's cyber-attacks on and manipulation of Western Governments and particularly the US Presidential Election, read Craig Unger's masterful book "House of Trump – House of Putin" **(vi)** or "Moneyland – Why Thieves and Crooks now rule the world & How to take it back" by Oliver Bullough **(vii)**. Whilst all this enemy activity takes place the spiritual life of our nation is being wrecked. Our own media also doesn't help by influencing many to try the narcissistic and hedonistic lifestyle of the TV 'Made in Chelsea' characters, and irresponsible sports stars and Hollywood celebrities.

The Independent's Middle East Correspondent Patrick Coburn in Syria wrote about Raqqa: Headline: **Liberated'**

former Isis capital still gripped by fear, full of booby traps and bombed to oblivion. He goes on to say of the Wars in Syria: that unlike other Syrian cities bombed or shelled to the ground – and even in Mosul in Iraq – there is at least one district that has survived intact. When he returned however, to Raqqa four months after Isis was driven out of its 'capital', he found that this is no longer the case. The city's destruction was total! The reason for the Syrian and Russian air forces bombardment of Syrian people might now be seen in the massive migration of Moslems to the EU and the subsequent destabilization of Europe. Many commentators believe that this has been a deliberate plan by Moscow in order to destabilize Europe! If that upsets you, then take a breath and consider the evil plan of the United Nations to move over fifty-nine million Africans and Middle East citizens in a forced migration to Europe. You might ask why. The answer is because in their mind numbingly cerebral emptiness they believe that Europe and the West need new blood to boost shrinking populations! Words fail me – here again is the United Nation (as it plans to call itself) playing the One World Government at the expense and without the knowledge of ordinary people. God used the Prophet Nahum to tell Assyria and its capital city Nineveh, that they due to their evil, they were finished, and their place would be known no more. Within a short time that promise became true and travelers walked over the hidden ruins of Ninevah. Only God can do that. The UN cannot save Europe, even though they are trying but the same fate will come to Europe and America shortly, when Jesus returns.

For these reasons just outlined, I think that our political landscape is looking more like a Patrick Coburn report from Syria – our society is ruined and littered with the debris and ruins of former political, social, religious and spiritual landmarks. This is war – spiritual war for the lives of our population. What we are seeing more and more is a breakdown in our society, a disconnect between the rich, political class and powerful and the ordinary man and woman. We are seeing a battle between competing religions for the life of the nation and waiting in the wings, international predators ready to destroy our Judaeo-Christian heritage, culture and liberal democratic values. I think that I have some empathy with Moses when God commended him to speak to the Children of Israel and say that they had to decide between life or death between blessings or curses (Deuteronomy 28).

But this Farewell Speech of Moses did not end with the Curses. It continued. Here is how Moses made his final pronouncement. *"When all these blessings and curses I have set before you come on you and you take them to heart wherever the LORD your God disperses you among the nations, and when you and your children return to the LORD your God and obey him with all your heart and with all your soul according to everything I command you today, then the LORD your God will restore your fortunes and have compassion on you and gather you again from all the nations where he scattered you. Even if you have been banished to the most distant land under the heavens, from there the LORD your God will gather you and bring you back. He will bring you to the land that belonged to your ancestors, and you will take possession of it. He will make you more prosperous and numerous than your ancestors."* (Deuteronomy 30:1-5) The late Derek Prince wrote a superb study on this entitled "Blessing or Curse – You can choose! **(viii)**

End Notes:
i.   **Great Britain has Fallen** – Wale Babatunde: New Wine Press
ii. **God's Glorious Promise** – Andrew Baguley and Roger French: New Wine Press
iii. **Shaken** – Andrew Baguley – New Wine Press
iv. **Where are we heading? Heaven only knows** – Andrew Baguley: Lighthouse Publishing

Introduction

v. **Brief Answers to the Big Questions** – Stephen Hawking: John Murray 2018
vi. **House of Trump, House of Putin** – Craig Unger: Bantam Press
vii. **Moneyland, Why thieves and crooks now rule the world & How to take it back** – Oliver Bullough: Profile Books
viii. **Blessing or Curse – You Can Choose!** – Derek Prince: Derek Prince Ministries

19

CHAPTER ONE

Testimonies of heaven and hell

*"Man is destined to die once, and after
that to face judgement"* Hebrews 9:27

*"For the wages of sin is death, but the gift of
God is eternal life in Christ Jesus our Lord"*
Romans 6:23

The Bible clearly teaches that there is a divide between the
believer and the unbeliever: Outside of Jesus Christ the
unbeliever has no way of overcoming the problem of sin
and the resulting judgement of God. How wonderful that the
Apostle Paul could write to the Philippian Church *"for to me, to
live is Christ and to die is gain"* (Philippians 1:21 NIV)

In this first chapter of the book we are introduced to heaven
and hell through the life and death experiences of two people.
One a young girl and one a young man. We begin with the
young girl using her mother's written testimony.

Miracles from Heaven: Christy Wilson Beam **(i)**

This is a testimony about a little girl's life and that of her parents
and sibling affected by an incurable, life threatening digestive
disorder, who on a rare day of good health falls head first down
the inside of a thirty-foot deep hollow tree whilst climbing with

her sister. Her parents ranch in Texas was some distance from medical facilities and services. She lay silent and unmoving curled up in the foetal position for a long time before she could be rescued and transferred to an ambulance. Annabel had a childlike faith in God and shared with her parents their Christian faith and attended Sunday School with her sisters when she was well. There is no doubt that their Christian faith held the family together during some very dark times.

Christy writes "our home was a happy one, despite the bumpy road. We laughed, we teased, we went places. It was hard to commit to extracurricular activities, but we did our best to keep the girls involved and active. Abby played softball and excelled in school. I enrolled all three girls in gymnastics. Every six weeks or so, Anna landed in the hospital for a few days. It became a way of life. Kevin and I had the routine down to a science. Abigail and Adelynn could run the obstacle course, from grabbing backpacks to buckling seat belts to hopping out at their host home. Our friends and family got used to seeing our number pop up on their caller ID at any and all hours. They were there for us at a moment's notice, morning, noon, and night."

As Annabel lay trapped at the bottom of the hollow tree, something amazing happened. In the days that followed she shared a stunning story of visiting heaven, meeting Jesus and being guided by the light of a guardian angel. But, as Christy writes "the greatest miracle of all had only just begun to unfold – a medical miracle that has left the medical specialists baffled. The morning after Annabel was rescued and taken to hospital, Christy went to the hospital with more clothes for her and with some spare clothes for her husband. When she entered Annabel's room she was greeted with the news that Annabel was free to go home because despite her medical record and history of regular surgery to remove obstructions in her intestines, and despite the injuries to her head and body as she fell within the hollow tree, the doctors could find nothing wrong with her!

In the car on the way home, Annabel explained to Christy what had happened to her. "You know . . . I went to heaven when I was sitting in that tree . . . I sat on Jesus lap." She explained in a matter of fact way what she saw in heaven, how the gates are made of gold, how Jesus told her it wasn't time, that she would have to go back and couldn't see the 'creatures'. When Jesus told her that He would send His guardian angel, Annabel started to wake up in the tree and hear the fireman's voices. She saw an angel that looked very small – like a fairy- and it got more and more clear. Then, she said, God winked at her through the angel as if saying to her "I'm going to leave you now, and everything is going to be okay." Everything was and is okay for the whole family who have enjoyed being a part of the miracle love of God.

The second account is that of a young man named Ian McCormack. Ian has travelled the world giving his testimony and Jenny Sharkey ahs written a book about it. The testimony is very long and so I have abridged it in order to concentrate upon the theme of this chapter. If you would like to read the full testimony then you can by either reading the book or by googling 'Ian McCormack Testimony' on line and following the links.

Ian McCormack's story – As told by Jenny Sharkey in her book "A Glimpse of Eternity" **(ii)**

"A Glimpse of Eternity" is the incredible true story of one man's encounter with death and the realms beyond it. Stung by five box jellyfish while diving off the coast of Mauritius, Ian McCormack later died in hospital and was dead for 15-20 minutes. During this time he experienced both hell and heaven and came back to tell the story! Dying was his doorway to true life and his story is transforming lives around the world as it touches on some of the deepest questions, we all eventually ask.

"It was 1980 and I was 24 years old when I set out on an adventure that was to turn my life upside down. I had saved some money and was eager to travel and explore the world. My best friend and I decided to sell our worldly possessions and head out on a surfing safari, an 'endless summer' holiday.

So off I went with my surfboard under my arm. I initially flew to Sydney, Australia first and surfed my way up the East Coast of Australia to Surfers Paradise. I travelled light and stayed in the cheapest accommodation I could find, while spending my days catching good waves at Dee Why, Fosters, Lennox Heads, Byron Bay and Burleigh Heads.

I hitchhiked up through the outback of Australia to Darwin and then carried on to Bali in Indonesia, where I surfed Kuta Reef, then took my chances surfing Uluwatu, an amazing left-hand reef break. I also visited a few Hindu & Buddhist temple sites before continuing on overland through Java.

As I travelled through Asia the people often asked me if I was a Christian, presumably because I was white skinned. The question challenged me because I had been brought up in a Christian family, but I wasn't sure if I should call myself a Christian.

I was raised as an Anglican and attended the "Church of England". At the age of 14 years I was confirmed in the church. I would pray as a child, and went to Sunday school and youth group, and yet I'd never really had a personal experience with God. I remember coming out of the church on the day of my confirmation quite disillusioned. Nothing seemed to have happened. My heart was full of questions, so I asked my mother if God had ever spoken personally to her. She turned to me and said, "God does speak, and He is real". Then she shared how she had cried out to God in a time of tragedy and He had answered her. So, I asked her why God hadn't ever spoken to me. I vividly remember her answer; "Often it takes a tragedy to humble us so that we will turn to God. Men by nature tend to be quite proud". I retorted, "I'm not that kind of person, I'm not proud". But when I reflect on it, I was very proud.

My mother said, "I'm not going to force you to come to church. But remember this one thing. Whatever you do in life, wherever you go, no matter how far you think you've gone away from God, remember this one thing; if you're in trouble and in need, cry out to God from your heart, and he will hear you. He will really hear you and forgive you." I remembered those words. They stuck in my mind. But I decided that rather than be a hypocrite I wouldn't go back to church because I had never really had an experience with God. It was basically just religion to me.

I travelled on up through Java, Singapore, Tiomen Island and into Malaysia, then onto Colombo, Sri Lanka with a Dutch woman I had met up with. Once there, I made my way up the coast to surf Arugum Bay. After a month of awesome waves my visa was running out, so I returned to Colombo.

I befriended some Tamil people in Colombo who welcomed me into their home and family life. One time while I was staying with them, we all travelled to the hidden city of Katragarma. While I was at this sacred city, I had my first supernatural experience. As I was looking at a carved idol, I actually saw its lips move. I was deeply disturbed by this experience and I wanted to get out of that place as soon as I could!

As I continued to live with my Tamil friends, I observed that each day they would offer food to their household idol, the elephant god Garnesh. Some days they would clothe it, other days bath it in milk or water. It seemed strange to me that a person could believe a stone idol could be a god, as someone had obviously made it with their own hands. But looking at that stone statue one day I felt an evil yet powerful presence emanating from it. It surprised and intimidated me. Then into my mind these words came, "You shall have no other God but me and you shall not bow down to any graven image or idol." Immediately I realised that this was one of the Ten Commandments found in the Bible (Exodus 20:4-5) and I began to reflect on these words that I had heard way back at Sunday school.

I eventually returned to Arugam Bay where I was excited to get a crewing position on a 27-metre schooner called the "Constellation". We sailed out of Sri Lanka in the middle of the night en route for Africa and twenty-six days later, after many sea adventures, we arrived in Port Louis harbour on the island of Mauritius.

While I was in Mauritius I lived in Tamarin Bay among the local Creole fishermen and surfers. Hashish (Marijuana) gave us a common bond and they accepted me into their lives and taught me to night- dive on the outer reefs. Night diving is an incredible experience. The crayfish come out at night and you can blind them with your under-water flashlight and just pick them up. The fish go to sleep at night and you only need to decide which one you want to spear for dinner. It was a fantastic sport and we would sell our catches to the local tourist hotel.

After surfing my heart out on Tamarin's very fast left-hand reef break for several weeks, I was running out of money. So, I headed to South Africa where I found a job teaching windsurfing and water-skiing. Amazingly they actually paid me to do this! I surfed Jeffrey's Bay and Elands Bay and visited some of South Africa's world- famous wildlife reservations.

At my stopover in Reunion I found an amazing surf break called St Leu where I had some great waves to myself. Then I headed on to Mauritius. It was March 1982 and I'd been travelling now for nearly two years, often sleeping in a tent on beaches and living like a nomad. It was time to return home.

Back in Mauritius again for a few weeks, I rented a house, reconnected with my Creole friends, and spent my time surfing and night diving. One evening a week before I was due to leave for New Zealand, a diving friend came to my house and asked me to come out night diving with him. I walked out onto my veranda and saw a huge electrical storm raging out at sea.

The white electric lightning flashes were illuminating the black sky. I turned to my friend Simon and asked, "Are you sure – have you seen the storm?" I was afraid the storm would bring too much surf up onto the reef and become dangerous. But Simon replied "It'll be okay, we'll go about five miles down the coast to a very beautiful part of the reef to dive tonight. You'll be amazed how beautiful it is."

In the end he talked me into it. It was about 11 o'clock at night. I got all my gear, jumped in the boat and off we all went – Simon, another local diver, a boat boy, and myself. We rowed down the coast to the spot that Simon had talked about. We were about half a mile off the actual island. The boat was sitting in the inner lagoon, and we were going to dive on the outer part of the reef where it drops away steeply into the ocean. It really was as beautiful as Simon had said it would be.

We dived in. I went up the reef and my two friends went down the reef. Normally we stick together but for some reason we got separated. I was looking for crayfish when my flashlight beam picked out a strange sea creature in the dark water. It looked like a squid. Curious, I swam closer to it and reached out my hand and grabbed it. I had my diving gloves on and it squeezed through my fingers like a jellyfish. As it floated away I watched it, intrigued, as it was a very odd-looking jellyfish. It had what appeared to be a squid's bell-shaped head, but its back was box shaped and it had very unusual, transparent, finger like tentacles stretching way out behind it. I'd never seen that type of jellyfish before, but I turned away from it and continued with my crayfish search.

I turned my flashlight back onto the reef and continued searching for my prey. Suddenly something smashed into my forearm like a thousand volts of electricity. I swung around to see what it was. I had a short arm wetsuit on, so the only part of my body that wasn't covered by a wetsuit was my forearms. Something had brushed past me and stung me with an incredible shock. It was like standing on wet concrete, bare foot, and resting your hand right up against the electrical mains. I recoiled from it in fright and searched frantically with my flashlight to find out what it was, or where it was, but I couldn't see what had hit me.

Maybe something had bitten me, or I'd cut myself on the reef. I looked down at my arm to see if there was any blood, but there was nothing, just a throbbing pain. I rubbed it, which turned out to be one of the worst things I could have done as it served to rub the poison into my bloodstream. By now the pain seemed to be numbing out a bit so I thought, "I'll just get a crayfish and then I'll go back and ask the boy at the boat what it was." I didn't want to get paranoid; I knew it was very important for my own safety as a diver not to panic.

So, I went to get a crayfish. As I was diving under again, I saw these same jellyfish creatures that I'd seen a few minutes ago. Two of them were slowly, eerily, pulsating towards me with their long tentacles swirling behind them. Out of the corner of my eye I saw their tentacles brush past my arm. As they touched my arm, I was again jolted by an incredible electric shock. It just about knocked me for a six in the water. I suddenly realised what it was that had hit me the first time!

I knew from my lifesaving experience that some jellyfish are incredibly poisonous. As a child I had hay fever and had such bad allergic reactions that if I got stung by a bee my leg would swell up like a balloon. Now I began feeling alarmed because I'd had two separate stings from these jellyfish. I broke the surface of the water, gasping for air, and lifted my head to look for the boat. The storm clouds were settling in and making everything dark. I could just make the boat out further down the reef. I put my arm behind my back to get it out of the water. I didn't want it to be stung again. Then I began to swim in the direction of the reef, trying to fight off the terror I was feeling. As I swam, I felt something slide over my back and then another huge shock pulsed through my arm. Looking round I saw tentacles falling off. I'd been stung by a third one!

Finally, I made it back to the boat where I desperately questioned the young boy in my best French and Creole, asking if he knew what the jellyfish were. He didn't know because he wasn't a diver, he just shook his head and he pointed to my friend Simon in the water. So, I had to get back into the water and swim over to him. I could see him underwater, so I flashed my light into his face to get his attention. He came up to the surface, and I exclaimed to him "I want to get out!" I put my head into the water to swim back to the boat and right in front of my face there was another jellyfish surging at me. I had to choose, it was either going to hit my face or my arm. So, I lifted my arm up and took another agonising sting to my arm as I pushed it away. Then I struggled out on to the reef.

Two feet of water covered the actual reef. I stood there in my flippers and looked at my arm, which was literally swollen like a balloon with lesions across the top of the skin like burn blisters. It was as though I'd burnt it on a stove, right across where the tentacles had been dragged.

As I was looking at it, my friend Simon came walking across the reef in his flippers towards me. He was wearing a full wetsuit, as they all did because they were brought up in the tropics and the water felt cold to them. He looked at my arm, and then he looked at me. He asked breathlessly, "How many? How many times have you been stung?" I answered, "Four I think." He said, "Invisible? Was it transparent?" I replied, "Yeah, it looks invisible." Simon hung his head down and swore. He said "One sting and you're finished, just one!" He put his flashlight up to his face and I could see written there the seriousness of the situation. I said "Well, what am I doing with four of them on my arm then?" "You've got to go to the hospital." He said, "Aller, aller, vite." The main hospital was 15 miles away, it was the middle of the night and I was half a mile out to sea on a reef. I could hear him say "go" but I felt paralysed standing there. He was trying to get me back into the boat. As he dragged me in I realised that my right arm was literally paralysed, and I couldn't lift it up out of the water. At that point, as I was trying to drag my arm up out of the water into the boat a fifth jellyfish swam across it and added another lesion to my already disfigured forearm.

In my heart I thought, "What have I done to deserve this?" Then I got a flashback of my sin. I knew instantly what I'd done wrong. There were plenty of things I had done to deserve this. You don't get away with anything.

My two friends lifted the boat over the reef with me in it. It was ripping the bottom. It was a wooden boat, and the boat was their livelihood, so I knew the situation was very serious for them to be doing that. They lifted the boat over into the lagoon and were swimming, trying to push the boat to get it going. I said, "Come with me!" But they replied, "No, it's too heavy, get the young boy to take you ashore". So this young kid was pushing the boat to shore with a pole.

I felt like I was on fire. I could feel the poison going through my blood stream and it punched at something under my arm. A lymph gland was being hit. It was becoming increasingly difficult for me to breathe into my right lung. My right lung was being constricted by my wetsuit, so I undid my wetsuit with my left arm, peeled it off and put on my trousers while I could still move. My mouth was dry, and I sat there dripping with perspiration. I could feel the poison moving. I could feel a sharp pain in my back as if someone had hit me in the kidneys. I was trying not to move, trying not to panic. We were only half way to shore and I could literally feel the poison pulsating and moving through my blood system.

I didn't know what direction my blood went in until that night, but I tell you what, I became really interested in which way my blood circulated! The poison was now numbing out the whole of my right leg, and I had enough common sense to know that if it got down that leg and back up to my heart or my brain, then I was dead. As I was coming to shore, my vision was blurring. I was finding it difficult to focus. We reached the shore and I stood up to get out of the boat and my right leg crumbled underneath me. I fell right onto the crayfish in the bottom of the boat. The young boy stood back a bit shocked, then he motioned for me to put my arm around his neck. I put my arm around his neck, grabbed my paralysed arm with my good arm and just held on. He dragged me out of the boat and then up the beach on the coral sand. He got me up onto the main road.

It was about midnight. The place was desolate - no cars, no nothing. I was holding on to the young boy wondering how on earth I was going to get from there to the hospital at such a late time of the night. I was so weak in my right leg that I sat down on the tarmac. The young boy tried to help me but in the end he started pointing to the ocean again saying, "My brothers, I need to get them". I said, "No, stay here and help me." I knew the others could safely swim in from the reef because the jellyfish were on the outside of the reef. But he took off, and I was left alone on the side of the road in the middle of the night. Hope drained from me and I lay down to rest.

Tiredness overwhelmed me as I stared up into the stars. I was just about to close my eyes and go to sleep, when I heard a clear voice speak to me, and say "Ian, if you close your eyes you shall never awake again". I looked around expecting to see a man standing there but I saw no-one. It startled me and I shook off the sleepiness and thought, "What am I doing? I can't go to sleep here, I need to get to a hospital, I need to get anti-toxins, and I need to get help. If I go to sleep here I may actually never wake up."

So I tried to stand again. I was able to hobble slowly down the road and I found a couple of taxis parked at a petrol station next to a restaurant. I limped over to the taxis and begged the drivers to take me to the hospital. The men in the cars looked at me and said, "How much money will you pay us?" So I said, "I haven't got any money" – speaking out loud to myself. Then I realised what a foolish thing it was to admit to these men that I had no money. I could have lied, but I didn't, I just told the truth. I have no money. And the three drivers just laughed, "You're drunk, you're crazy". They turned around, lit their cigarettes and started to walk off.

Then I heard a clear voice again say "Ian, are you willing to beg for your life?" I sure was! And I even knew how to do it. It was very easy for me to get down on my knees because my right leg was already paralysed, and my left leg was very wobbly. I was leaning up against the car, so I just slipped down on to my knees and cupped my hands. Lowering my head so as not to look at them I begged for my life. I was nearly crying. I knew that if I didn't get to hospital soon then I wasn't going anywhere. If these guys didn't have compassion and love in their heart for me, and mercy towards me, I would have died right there in front of them.

So, I begged and pleaded with them for my life. With my head bent I watched their feet. Two of them just walked away, but I could see one young man moving his feet in indecision. It seemed to go on for an unbearably long time, but then he come over and picked me up. He didn't speak but he helped me up, put me in the car and drove off. Half way to the hospital however, he changed his mind. He demanded "What hotel you stay in white man?" I replied that I didn't live in a hotel but in a bungalow at Tamarin Bay. He thought I had lied to him and was angry that he might not get any money from me after all. "How will I get my money?" he retorted. I answered, "I'll give you all the money I've got!" When your life's at stake, money means nothing. I said "I'll give you any money you want if you can get me to hospital. I'll give you it all." But he didn't believe me. So, he changed his mind and took me to a big tourist hotel. He said, "I'll drop you here; I'm not going to take you." I pleaded with him to take me, but he leaned over, undid my safety belt and opened the door. "Get out!" he demanded. But I couldn't get out, I could barely move. So, he just shoved me out.

My legs caught on the doorsill, so he lifted them up and pushed them out, slammed the door and drove off. I lay there, and thought, "This world stinks. I've seen death, hatred, violence; this is hell, this place is hell on earth. This is a filthy, sick world we live in." I lay there, and I felt like giving up. I thought, "What's the point of even trying to get to hospital? If your number's up let it go, just die."

Then my grandfather came to mind. He went through the First and Second World Wars. He'd been to Gallipoli and had fought in Egypt against Rommel. I remembered this and thought how my Granddad had survived two world wars and here was his grandson giving up because five miserable jellyfish had stung him! So, I thought, "I'll go to the last breath, don't give up yet Ian!" Using my one remaining working arm I tried to drag myself towards the hotel entrance. I could see some lights on. To my amazement the security guards were doing the rounds and their flashlights spotted me grovelling along in the dirt.

A man came running over. I looked up and recognised him to be one of my drinking friends. He was a black guy called Daniel, a big lovable man. He came running up to me and asked, "What's wrong with you, are you drunk, are you stoned, what's wrong with you?" I pulled up my sweatshirt to show him my arm and he could see all the blisters and the swollenness. He scooped me up in his arms and ran.

It was like having an angel pick me up. He ran in, past the swimming pool and dropped me into a cane chair. About three metres away the Chinese hotel owners were playing mah-jong and drinking. All the tourists had gone to bed, the bar was closed but they were still gambling.

Daniel dropped me there and disappeared into the darkness again. I wondered where he had gone but then I realised that a black man couldn't speak to a Chinese man in this country unless he is asked to speak. I was going to have to try and communicate to these Chinese men myself. So, I pulled up my sleeve and showed them my swollen and blistered limb. I said, "I need to go to 'Quartre Bonne' hospital immediately, I've been stung by five jellyfish." I even used some Chinese. They laughed. One of the young men got up and said, "Oh white boy, heroin no good for you, only old men take the Opium." He thought I was on drugs because I showed him my arm and from that distance it looked like I had injected myself.

I was becoming furious and frustrated by this. I sat there trying to keep myself calm, because I knew that if I got too excited the poison would move quicker. My right hand started to shake. It was twitching strangely between my knuckles, in spasms. The twitching came up my arm and into my face and my teeth began chattering. Soon my whole body, every muscle, started to twitch and contract with the death shakes. I was literally leaving my seat with each contraction as the poison was reacting with my muscles. The Chinese men came running over and three men tried to hold me down. They couldn't contain me; I was throwing them off.

When I came out of this incredible shaking a deadly cold crept over my bone marrow. I could literally see a darkness creeping over the inner part of my bone. It was like death creeping over me. I knew my body was dying, right before my eyes. I was incredibly cold.

The men started putting blankets all over me trying to keep me warm. One of them tried to pour milk down my throat, presuming I had swallowed toxin. I could see one vehicle in the hotel carpark. I knew which man it belonged as he had often driven past me and sounded his horn when I had hitchhiked from place to place. I pleaded with him to take me in his car to the hospital, but he answered, "No, we wait for ambulance white boy." I was so mad I wanted to hit him, but I couldn't move either of my arms. I wondered if I could head-butt him, but I realised that the adrenaline it would use might kill me.

So, I sat there thinking, "I don't think I'm ever going to get there." Just then the ambulance arrived and out of nowhere Daniel appeared with another security man. They picked me up in their arms and took off. I realised then that Daniel had initially gone straight to the switchboard and phoned the hospital himself.

The ambulance came screaming in with its headlights sweeping the carpark, did a U-turn in front of the hotel, and took off again! The ambulance driver was from a black hospital, so when there was no one at the front of the Chinese hotel to collect he obviously thought he had his instructions wrong.

So, there I was, desperate, half way to the gates, and I could see the ambulance disappearing around the corner. I tried to whistle but my mouth was so parched that I couldn't get a sound out. Daniel saw what I was trying to do so he wolf whistled as loud as he could. It ricocheted off the wall and down the road. The ambulance driver must have had his window down because the red brake lights came on and to my great relief he backed up. The ambulance was an old Renault 4 with a front seat taken out and a camp stretcher put in its place. That's it boys, that's the ambulance!

We were half way to the hospital and the Renault was climbing a hill. My feet were going up in the air and the poison in my blood was starting to rush straight to my brain. I started seeing a picture of a little snowy-headed boy, and then I saw another flash of an older boy with snowy white hair. I was looking at this picture thinking, "Gee, he's got white hair," and it suddenly occurred to me that I was looking at myself, that I was seeing my life go before me. It was a frightening experience watching these pictures of my life in front of me like a video playing, clear as crystal with my eyes wide open. I looked and thought, "I've heard about this, and I've even read about it. People say just before they die their life flashes before them."

I said to myself, "I'm too young to die, why did I go diving? What an idiot, I should have stayed at home." My thoughts were racing. Now I knew I was confronted with imminent death. I could hardly hear my heart beat and I lay there wondering what would happen if I died? Is there anything after I die? Where would I go if I died?

Then I saw a clear vision of my mother. It was as though she was speaking out those words she had spoken so long ago; "Ian, no matter how far from God you are, no matter what you've done wrong, if you cry out to God from your heart, he will hear you and he will forgive you."

In my heart I was thinking, "Do I believe there is a God? Am I going to pray?" I'd almost become a devout atheist. I didn't believe anybody. Yet, I was confronted by this vision of my mother. I talked with my mother about this later when I returned to New Zealand. She said she had been woken in the early hours of that same morning. God had shown her my blood shot eyes and said to her," your eldest son Ian is nearly dead. Pray for him now." So, she had been praying for me at that very moment that I lay dying in the ambulance.

Now of course her prayers couldn't save my soul, she couldn't get me to heaven, but I knew at that moment that I needed to pray. Only I didn't know what to pray or who to pray to. Which god should I pray to? Buddha, Kali, Shiva? There are thousands of them. Yet I didn't see Buddha or Krishna or some other god or man standing there, I saw my mother - and my mother follows Jesus Christ. I thought, "I haven't prayed for years, what should I pray? What do you pray at this point? What's the prayer if you're about to die?"

Then I remembered that as a child my mother taught us the 'Lord's prayer'. "Our Father who is in heaven, holy be your name, your kingdom come, your will be done on earth as it is in heaven . . ." I knew it as a child – I used to race my siblings each night to say it the fastest! That was the only prayer I knew. I started to pray it, but I couldn't remember it. It was as though the poison that had rushed to my head had inhibited my thinking ability. It was closing my mind down. It was terrifying. I had relied so much on my mind and my intellect and now suddenly it was dying on me. Mental blank, zero.

As I was lying there I remember my mother saying that you don't pray from your head, you pray from your heart. So, I said "God I want to pray – help me." As I said that, this prayer literally came up from my inner man, from my spirit. I prayed, "Forgive us our sins." Then I went on "God, I ask you to forgive my sins, but I have done so many things wrong. I know they're wrong, my conscience tells me they're wrong. If you can forgive me all my sins, and I don't know how you can do it – I've got no idea how you can forgive them – please forgive me of my sins". And I meant it. I wanted to wipe the slate clean, start again. "God forgive me."

As I prayed that, I got another part of the prayer. "Forgive those who have sinned against you." I understood that that meant I had to forgive those who had hurt me. I thought, "Well I don't hold grudges. There are heaps of people that have ripped me off and back-stabbed me and said bad things against me and done terrible things to me – I forgive them." Then I heard the voice of God say, "Will you forgive the Indian that pushed you out of the car and the Chinese men that wouldn't take you to the hospital?" I thought, "You must be joking! I had other plans for them!" But no more of the prayer would come. I knew I was in a catch 22 position. I thought, "Okay, I'll forgive them. If you can forgive me, I can forgive them. I will forgive them. I'll never lay a hand on them."

The next part of the prayer came to me, "Your will be done." I had done my own thing for the last 20 years. I said, "God, I don't even know what your will is – I know it's not to do evil things, but I've got no idea what your will is. If I come through this, I will find out your will for my life and I'll do it. I'll make a point of following you whole-heartedly if I come through this".

I didn't understand it at the time, but that was my prayer for salvation. Not from my head, but from my heart, asking "God forgive me for my wickedness and evil-doing. God cleanse me. I forgive all those that have hurt me. And Jesus Christ, I'll do your will – your will be done. I will follow you." I had prayed the sinner's prayer, the repentant prayer to God, and praying that prayer was pivotal to everything else that happened to me.

An incredible peace came over my heart. It seemed as though fear fell off me, the fear of what was coming. I was still dying, I knew that, but I was at peace about it. I'd made my peace with my Maker. I knew it, I knew for the first time that I'd touched God and I was actually hearing him. I'd never heard him before but now I was hearing him speaking to me. No one else could have told me the Lord's Prayer.

The ambulance turned off the road in to the hospital. Finally, I had made it! The driver lifted me into a wheelchair and ran me through to the emergency area. Someone took my blood pressure. As I was sitting there watching the nurse, she looked at the gauge and then she hit it. I thought, "What kind of hospital is this?" It was an old World-War Two army hospital. The British had deserted it and given it to the Creole people. It still looked like it was built in 1945. It was filthy and decrepit and yet there I was.

The nurse hit the gauge again. I began thinking, "There's nothing wrong with the machine, it's my heart – it's not pumping." She ripped off the gauge and rummaged through the cupboard, trying to find another one that looked newer. She pulled one out, slapped it on, opened it up and started pumping. I could see that whatever it was doing it was not registering very much. She looked at me, and then looked at the machine. My eyes were open, but I knew she was wondering why they were open. With this kind of blood pressure your eyes shouldn't be open. I was desperately hanging on. I was hanging on for all I was worth. I was fighting with all my strength to stay alive.

So, the ambulance driver, realising the situation was desperate, ripped the gauge off my arm and ran me through to the doctors. Two Indian doctors were sitting there, both of them half-asleep, heads down. "What's your name, where do you live?" One asked in French, "How old are you?" He was a young doctor and he didn't even look at me. I looked over to the older doctor. He had a bit of gray hair and I thought, "He's been around for a few years, he might know how to help me." So, I waited. The young doctor stopped talking and looked up. I didn't even bother looking at him but waited for the old man to lift his head up. He looked up. I wasn't sure if I had enough strength left to speak. I locked into his eyes and I gave him the heaviest look I could muster. I whispered, "I am about to die, I need anti-toxins right now". He didn't move. I didn't take my eyes off him, he was just staring straight back into them.

The nurse came in with a piece of paper. The older doctor looked at it, looked at me, and jumped. I could see him screw it up in disgust as if to say to the younger doctor, "You foolish idiot, why didn't you look at this young man?" He jumped up, pushed the ambulance driver out of the way, grabbed the wheelchair himself and started racing me down the corridor. I could hear a kind of muffled noise. I could hear him screaming out something but it was muffled to me.

The doctor ran into a room with bottles and medical equipment in it. Next minute I was surrounded by nurses, doctors and orderlies. At long last, something was happening. A nurse turned my arm over and put in a drip feed. The doctor was up near my face saying, "I don't know if you can hear me son but we're going to try and save your life. Keep your eyes open . . . come on son, fight the poison. Try and keep awake, we're putting dextrose in for dehydration." A nurse jabbed a needle in one side and another nurse was on the other side, jabbing. I couldn't feel them but I could see them doing it. The doctor was saying, "Anti-toxins to counteract the poison." in his Oxford English. Another nurse knelt by my feet, slapping my hand as hard as she could. I was thinking, "What is she doing?" But I didn't care, just shove the needles in! A nurse behind me was filling a huge syringe, like a horse syringe. She was squeezing the air out of it. She tried to stick it in my arm but no vein came up. So, she lifted my skin up, put the needle in and started pushing the liquid in. It filled up my vein like a small balloon. I could see how nervous she was because the needle was inside the vein and it looked like it was shaking so much that it would tear my vein open.

My heart was obviously not pumping around enough blood. My veins were collapsing. I'd done veterinary science in my degree, so I had studied and understood basic physiology and anatomy. I understood what was going on, but I couldn't do anything about it. I understood that I was slipping into a comatose state. I was totally paralysed, and my heart was barely pumping. As I was watching the needles, I felt myself slipping further and further away. I couldn't communicate any more, I couldn't say a thing, but I could still hear everything that was being said about and around me.

I had no idea that what I'd been stung by was a box jellyfish or a Sea-wasp. The box jellyfish exudes the second deadliest venom known to man. Being stung only once has killed up to 60 people in Darwin alone over the last 20 years. For six months of the year they put up a skull and cross bones sign on the beaches in Darwin to prevent bathers from going into the water to swim. I had enough toxins in me to kill me five times over. Normally a person dies within fifteen minutes of the initial sting and I didn't have it just on a muscle, I had it right across my veins.

The doctor looked me in the eye and said, "Don't be afraid." I thought, "Mate, you're more afraid than I am." I could see the paranoia in his eyes. I was lifted up and put on a bed with my drip feed. The doctor stood over me sponging my head. The drip feed they had put in my veins was bringing liquid back into my body and I was starting to perspire on my forehead. The doctor was wiping it from my face, but then he walked off for a few minutes. As I lay there I could feel it dripping into my eyes and it started to blur my vision, it was like tears coming into my eyes.

"I've got to keep my eyes open." I told myself. I willed the doctor to come back and wipe my face, but he didn't return. I tried to speak, "Doctor come back" but my lips would not move. I tried to tilt my head, but my head wouldn't move. So, I flicked it out with my eyelids. I squeezed a little out, but it was still blurry. I kept squeezing my eyelids shut. It worked a little, and then all of a sudden, I sighed, like a sigh of relief and I knew something had happened.

I knew I'd gone somewhere, it wasn't like closing your eyes and going to sleep, I knew I'd actually gone somewhere. For the previous 20 minutes in the hospital I had been feeling like I was floating away, and yet when I closed my eyes, I wasn't floating away – I was gone.

The Bible says in Ecclesiastes, that when a man dies his spirit returns to God who gave it and his body returns to the dust from which it came. Well, I knew my spirit had left, I had gone somewhere, and yet I didn't know I was dead. I seemed to arrive in a huge, broad place - like a cavernous hall of pitch-black darkness. I was standing up. It was as if I had woken up from a bad dream in someone else's house and was wondering where everyone had gone. I was trying to find the light switch, and I couldn't seem to find it. I wondered why the doctor had turned the lights out. I was trying to touch something, reaching for the wall lamp but I couldn't find it. Then I realised I couldn't find my bed. I was moving around but I wasn't bumping into anything. I couldn't see my hand in front of my face. It was bitterly cold. I strained to see where I was – trying to orient myself to these new surroundings.

I lifted my hand up to find out how much I could see. I lifted it to where my face was, and it went straight through where my face should have been. It was a terrifying experience. I knew right there and then, I was myself, Ian McCormack, standing there, but without a physical body. I had the sensation and the feeling that I had a body, but I couldn't touch it. I was a spiritual being, and my physical body had died, but I was very much alive, and very much aware that I had arms and legs and a head, but I could no longer touch them. God is a spirit, an invisible spiritual being, and we are created in his image.

"Where on earth am I?" I thought. As I was standing there in the darkness, I sensed the most incredible coldness and dread come over me. Maybe you've walked down a lonely street at night, or you've come home by yourself in the dark and you feel as though there is someone looking at you. Ever felt that? Well I began to sense evil encroaching on me in the darkness. The darkness seemed invasive. I knew I was being watched. A cold encroaching evil seemed to pervade the air around me.

Slowly I became aware that there were other people moving around me, in the same predicament as I was. Without my saying a word out loud, they began to answer my thoughts. From the darkness I heard a voice screaming at me: "Shut up!" As I backed away from that one another yelled at me, "You deserve to be here!" My arms came up to protect myself and I thought, "Where am I?" and a third voice shouted, "You're in hell. Now shut up." I was terrified – afraid to move or breathe or speak. I realised that maybe I did deserve this place.

People sometimes have this strange picture of hell being party time. I used to think that. I thought that in hell you would get to do all the things there that you're not supposed to do on earth. That is so far from the reality of it. The place I was in was the most frightening place I've ever been. The people there could not do anything that their wicked hearts wanted to do, they couldn't do anything. And there's no boasting. Who could you boast to down there? "Oh yeah, I raped, murdered, plundered, pillaged." There's nothing to talk about when you know that judgment is coming.

There is no relationship to time in that place. The people there can't tell what time it is. They can't tell whether they've been there ten minutes, ten years or 10,000 years. They had no relationship to time. It was a frightening place. The Bible says that there are two kingdoms, the Kingdom of Darkness, which is ruled by Satan, and the Kingdom of Light. The book of Jude says that the place of darkness was actually prepared for angels that disobeyed God, not for people, ever. And it was the scariest and the most frightening and the most terrifying place I have ever been in. I would never wish or hope that even my worst enemy went to hell.

I had no idea how to get out of that place. How do you ever get out of hell? But I had already prayed, and I was wondering why I'd gone there, because I'd prayed just before I died, and asked God to forgive me for my sins. I was weeping by now and I literally cried out to God, "Why am I here, I've asked you for forgiveness, why am I here? I've turned my heart to you, why am I here?"

Then a brilliant light shone upon me and literally drew me out of the darkness. The Bible says that a great light has shone into darkness, on those walking in the shadow of death and darkness and has guided their feet into the paths of peace and righteousness. As I stood there an amazing beam of light pierced through the darkness from above me and shone on my face. This light began to encompass me and a sense of weightlessness overwhelmed me. I lifted off the ground and begin to ascend up into this brilliant white light, like a speck of dust caught in a beam of sunlight.

As I looked up I could see I was being drawn into a large circular shaped opening far above me – a tunnel. I didn't want to look behind me in case I fell back into the darkness. I was very happy to be out of that darkness. Upon entering the tunnel I could see that the source of the light was emanating from the very end of the tunnel. It looked unspeakably bright, as if it was the centre of the universe, the source of all light and power. It was more brilliant than the sun, more radiant than any diamond, brighter than a laser beam light. Yet you could look right into it. As I looked, I was literally drawn to it, drawn like a moth into the presence of a flame. I was being pulled through the air at an amazing speed towards the end of the tunnel – towards the source of the light.

As I was being translated through the air I could see successive waves of thicker intensity light break off the source and start travelling up the tunnel towards me. The first wave of light gave off an amazing warmth and comfort. It was as though the light wasn't just material in nature but was a 'living light' that transmitted an emotion. The light passed into me and filled me with a sense of love and acceptance. Half way down another wave of light passed into me. This light gave off total and complete peace. I had looked for many years for 'peace of mind' but had only found fleeting moments of it. At school I had read from Keats to Shakespeare to try and get peace of mind. I had tried alcohol, I had tried education, I had tried sport, I had tried relationships with women, I had tried drugs, I tried everything I could think of to find peace and contentment in my life, and I'd never found it. Now from the top of my head to the base of my feet I found myself totally at peace.

My next thought was "I wonder what my body looks like?" In the darkness I hadn't been able to see my hands in front of my face. I thought "I must be able to see clearly now that I'm in this light." As I looked to my right to my amazement there was my arm and hand but I could see straight through them. I was transparent like a spirit, only my body was full of the same light that was shining on me from the end of the tunnel. It was as if I was full of light. The third wave near the end of the tunnel was total joy. It was so exciting that I knew that what I was about to see would be the most awesome experience in all my life.

My mind couldn't even conceive where I was going, and my words couldn't communicate what I saw. I came out of the end of the tunnel and seemed to be standing upright before the source of all the light and power. My whole vision was taken up with this incredible light. It looked like a white fire or a mountain of cut diamonds sparkling with the most indescribable brilliance. I immediately thought of it as aura, then as glory. I had seen pictures of Jesus with a little halo or small glow around his face, yet this glory was all encompassing, overwhelming, awe inspiring.

Jesus died to rescue us from the place I'd just come from, he rose from the dead and ascended into heaven, and he is now seated at the right-hand of the Father, and is glorified, surrounded by light and in him there is no darkness. He is the King of Glory, the Prince of Peace, the Lord of Lords and the King of all the Kings. I saw at that moment what I believe was the glory of the Lord. In the Old Testament, Moses went up Mount Sinai for 30 days and he saw the glory of the Lord. He came down and his face shone. Moses face shone so much with the glory of the Lord that he had to put on a veil, so that the people wouldn't be afraid. He had seen the light of God, the glory of God. Paul was blinded by a glorious light on the road to Damascus, the glory of Jesus. And I was now standing there seeing this incredible light and glory.

As I stood there, questions began racing through my heart; "Is this just a force, as the Buddhists say, or karma or Yin and Yang? Is this just some innate power or energy source or could there actually be someone standing in there?" I was still questioning it all.

As I thought these thoughts a voice spoke to me from the centre of the light. It was the same voice that I had heard earlier in the evening. The voice said, "Ian, do you wish to return?" I was shaken to learn that there was someone in the centre of the light and whoever it was knew my name. It was as though the person could hear my inner thoughts as speech. I then thought to myself "Return, return – to where? Where am I?" Quickly looking behind me I could see the tunnel dissipating back into darkness. I thought I must be in my hospital bed dreaming and I closed my eyes. "Is this real? Am I actually standing here, me, Ian, standing in real life here, is this real?" Then the Lord spoke again. "Do you wish to return?" I replied, "If I am out of my body I don't know where I am, I wish to return." The response was "If you wish to return Ian you must see in a new light."

The moment I heard the words "see in a new light," something clicked. I remembered being given a Christmas card, which said, "Jesus is the light of the world", and "God is light and there is no darkness in him." I had meditated upon those words at that time. I'd just come from darkness, and there was certainly no darkness here. I realised then that the light could be coming from God, and if it was – then what was I doing here? I didn't deserve to be here.

So this was God! He is light. He knew my name and he knew the secret thoughts of my heart and mind. I thought, "If this is God then he must also be able to see everything I've ever done in my life." I felt totally exposed and transparent before God. You can wear masks before other people, but you can't wear a mask before God. I felt ashamed and undone and I thought, "They've made a mistake and brought the wrong person up. I shouldn't be here. I'm not a very good person. I should crawl under some rock or go back into the darkness where I belong."

As I began to slowly move back towards the tunnel a wave of light emanated forth from God and moved towards me. My first thought was that this light was going to cast me back into the pit, but to my amazement a wave of pure unconditional love flowed over me. It was the last thing I expected. Instead of judgement I was being washed with pure love.

Pure, unadulterated, clean, uninhibited, undeserved, love. It began to fill me up from the inside out, making my hands and body tingle until I staggered. I thought, "Perhaps God doesn't know all the things I've done wrong," so I proceeded to tell him about all the disgusting things I'd done under the cover of darkness. But it was as though he'd already forgiven me, and the intensity of his love only increased. In fact, later God showed me that when I'd asked for forgiveness in the ambulance, it was then that he forgave me and washed my spirit clean from evil.

I found myself beginning to weep uncontrollably as the love became stronger and stronger. It was so clean and pure, no strings attached. I hadn't felt loved for years. The last time I remember being loved was by my mum and dad when I was at home, but I'd gone out into the big wide world and found out there's not too much love out there. I'd seen things that I thought were love, but sex wasn't love, it just burnt you up. Lust was like a raging fire inside you, an uncontrollable desire that burnt you up from the inside out. Yet this love was healing my heart and I began to understand that there is incredible hope for mankind in this love. God's mercy is always extended before his judgement.

As I stood there, the waves of light stopped, and I stood encased in pure light, filled with love. There was such stillness. I thought to myself, "I'm so close, I wonder if I could just step into the light that surrounds God and see him face to face. If I could see him face to face I will know the truth." I was sick of hearing lies and deceptions. I wanted to know the truth. I had been everywhere to find the truth, and no one seemed to be able to tell me. I would talk to anybody who could tell me the meaning to life – the truth – something had to be the truth. I thought if I could step through and meet God face-to-face I'll know the truth and I'll know the meaning to life. I will never have to ask another man, woman or child ever again. I'll know.

Could I step in? There was no voice saying I couldn't. So, I stepped through, I put my best foot forward and stepped through the light. As I stepped into the light it was as if I'd come inside veils of suspended shimmering lights, like suspended stars or diamonds giving off the most amazing radiance. And as I walked through the light it continued to heal the deepest part of me, it was healing my broken inner man, wonderfully healing my broken heart.

I aimed for the brightest part of the light. Standing in the centre of the light stood a man with dazzling white robes reaching down to his ankles. I could see his bare feet. The garments were not man-made fabrics but were like garments of light. As I lifted my eyes up I could see the chest of a man with his arms outstretched as if to welcome me. I looked towards his face. It was so bright; it seemed to be about ten times brighter than the light I'd already seen. It made the sun look yellow and pale in comparison. It was so bright that I couldn't make out the features of his face, and as I stood there I began to sense that the light was emitting purity and holiness. I knew that I was standing in the presence of Almighty God – no one but God could look like this. The purity and holiness continued to come forth from his face and I began to feel that purity and holiness enter into me. I wanted to get closer to see his face. I felt no fear but rather total freedom as I moved towards him. Standing now only a few feet from him, I tried to look into the light surrounding his face but as I did he moved to one side, and as he moved all the light moved with him.

Directly behind Jesus was a circular shaped opening like the tunnel I had just travelled down. Gazing out through it, I could see a whole new world opening up before me. I felt like I was standing on the edge of paradise, having a glimpse into eternity.

It was completely untouched. In front of me were green fields and meadows. The grass itself was giving off the same light and life that I had seen in the presence of God. There was no disease on the plants. It seemed as though the grass that it would just spring back to life if you stepped on it. Through the centre of the meadows I could see a crystal-clear stream winding its way across the landscape with trees on either bank. To my right were mountains in the distance and the sky above was blue and clear. To my left were rolling green hills and flowers, which were radiating beautiful colours. Paradise! I knew I belonged here. I had travelled the world looking for paradise, and here it was. I felt as though I had just been born for the first time. Every part of me knew I was home. Before me stood eternity – just one step away.

As I tried to step forward into this new world Jesus stepped back into the doorway. The Bible says that Jesus is the door and that if you come in through him, you will go in and out and find green pastures. He is the door to life. Jesus is the way, the truth and the life. No one comes to the Father but by him. He is the only way. There is only one narrow passageway that leads into his kingdom. Few find it. Most find the highway down to hell.

Jesus asked me this question "Ian, now that you have seen do you wish to return?" I thought, "Return, of course not. Why would I want to go back? Why would I want to return to the misery and hatred? No, I have nothing to return for. I have no wife or kids, no one who really loves me. You are the first person who has ever truly loved me as I am. I want to stay in your presence forever. I wish to go on in to paradise." But he didn't move so I looked back one last time to say, "Goodbye cruel world I'm out of here!"

As I did, in a clear vision right in front of the tunnel, stood my mother. As I saw her I knew I had just lied; there was one person who loved me – my dear Mum. Not only had she loved me, but also I knew she had prayed for me every day of my life, and she had tried to show me God. In my pride and arrogance, I had mocked her beliefs. But she had been right, there was a God and a heaven and a hell. I realised how selfish it would be to go through to paradise and leave my mother believing that I had gone to hell. She would have no idea that I'd made a deathbed prayer and repented of my sins and received Jesus as my Lord and Saviour. She would have just received a dead body in a box from Mauritius.

So I said, "God, there's only one person really I want to go back for and that is my mum. I want to tell her that what she believes in is true, that there is a living God, that there is a heaven and a hell, that there is a door and Jesus Christ is that door and that we can only come through him". Then as I looked back again, I saw behind her my father, my brother and sister, my friends, and a multitude of people behind them. God was showing me that there were a lot of other people who also didn't know and would never know unless I was able to share with them. I asked, "Who are all those other people?" And God said, "If you don't return, many of these people will not get an opportunity to hear about me because many will not put their foot inside a church". I responded, "I don't love those people" but he replied, "Son, I love them, and I desire all of them to come to know me."

Then the Lord said, "If you return you must see things in a new light." I understood that I must now see through his eyes, his eyes of love and forgiveness. I needed to see the world as he saw it – through the eyes of eternity. "God, how do I return?" I asked, "Do I have to go back through the tunnel of darkness, back into my body? How can I go back? I don't even know how I got here." He said, "Ian tilt your head . . . now feel liquid drain from your eyes . . . now open your eyes and see."

Immediately I was back in my body. My head was tilted to the right and I had one eye open. I was looking at a young Indian doctor who had my right foot elevated in his hand and was prodding a sharp instrument into the base of my foot. He was looking for any signs of life. Little did he realise that I was now alive and looking at him. I wondered what on earth he was doing but then the penny dropped; "He thinks I'm dead!" At the same time the doctor stopped what he was doing and turned his head in the direction of my face. As our eyes made contact, terror swept over his face, as though he had just seen a ghost. Blood drained from his face and he went as white as a sheet. His feet nearly left the ground.

I was shaken I asked God to give me the strength to tilt my head to the left and look out the other side. As I slowly turned my head to the left I saw nurses and orderlies in the doorway staring at me in amazement and terror. No one said a word. I apparently had been dead for some 15 to 20 minutes and was being prepared for the morgue. I felt weak and I closed my eyes, but I quickly opened them again to check that I was still in my body. I wasn't sure whether or not I would disappear again.

I was still paralysed, and I asked God to help me. As I prayed I felt a tingling sensation in my legs, accompanied by a comforting warmth. I continued to pray and the doctor just stood there shaking his head. The warmth spread up into my body and arms. God was healing me! I was so tired. I closed my eyes again and fell soundly asleep.

I didn't wake again until the next afternoon. When I woke I saw my friend Simon standing outside my room looking in through the window. He looked pale and was shaking his head. He couldn't believe I was alive. He had followed my trail to the hospital and had brought a New Zealand friend of mine with him. "So, you had a pretty rough night aye?" this friend asked. "Yeah mate" I replied, "I don't really know what happened." I didn't want to say, "Actually – I died!" I was still coming to terms with all that had happened and didn't want them to say, "Off to the rubber room for you – you've taken too much dope and it's coming out your ear-holes!"

"This place smells like a latrine." They said. "We're getting you out of here. We'll look after you." I resisted them – I wanted to stay in the hospital, but they climbed in the window, picked me up, put me over their shoulders and walked me out.

The doctor came and tried to physically restrain them but they pushed him out of their way. A taxi was waiting. Simon wouldn't come in the taxi with me as he was still afraid that I was a ghost. They took me home to my bungalow on the beach and put me to bed. Then they went straight out to the living room and had a party!

I was exhausted and hungry. I went to sleep again and woke up in the middle of the night shivering and perspiring. My heart was filled with terror. I was lying facing the wall. I rolled over to see what was scaring me. Through my mosquito netting and through the steel bars on the windows I could see seven or eight pairs of eyes looking at me. There was a light red glow to them. Instead of a round pupil they had slits like a cat. They seemed half human, half animal. I thought, "What on earth are they?" They looked into my eyes and I looked into theirs and I heard a whisper, "You're ours and we're coming back." "No you're not!" I cried. I grabbed my flashlight and shone it at them. There was nothing there – but I knew I'd seen them!

I wondered if I was going crazy. I began feeling like I might mentally snap. I had to settle myself down and convince myself I wasn't going insane. I'd been through so much in the last 24 hours. So, I said, "God, what's going on?" Then he took me inch by inch through everything I'd been through. It was as if he seared it onto my mind. At the end of this I asked him," what are these things that seem to want to attack me?" He replied, "Ian, remember the Lord's prayer". I tried to remember it with my mind again, but I couldn't. Then up from my heart came all the words through to "deliver me from the evil one". I prayed this earnestly from my heart. Then God said, "Turn the lights out Ian." I gathered up my courage and turned off the main light. I sat on the edge of my bed with my flashlight on. I felt like a Jedi warrior from Star Wars! I began thinking, "If I don't turn my flashlight out I'm going to have to spend the rest of my life sleeping with the light on." I turned the flashlight off.

Nothing happened. The prayer had been effective. I lay down and went to sleep.

The next morning I got up and prepared myself breakfast. My friends came in from their morning surf and began talking to me. I began seeing that what they were saying wasn't what they were actually meaning. It confused me, as if I was hearing two different messages. I began to see through their masks. For the first time in my life I was beginning to see things in a new light. I could see that the intents of their hearts were totally contrary to what was coming out of their mouths. It was frightening for me because I didn't know how to react to that kind of understanding. So, I retreated to my bedroom, and stayed there.

That night I woke again in a cold sweat. Something nearby was scaring me. I turned my head to look and to my horror, the demons I had seen last night were now in my bedroom looking at me through my mosquito net. Yet for some reason they couldn't get to me. They were intimidating me but they couldn't actually get to me. In my heart I had a deep peace. I knew I had seen the light of God and that light was now in me. No matter how small the flame was, it was in me and they couldn't come in. But they were certainly trying to terrify me and get me back.

I grabbed my flashlight again. This time I was afraid to get out of bed to turn on the light because they were in my room. I didn't know what power they had. I flashed the light madly around the room, leaped out of bed and dashed to the light-switch. With the light safely on I fell to the floor on my knees. I battled with my mind all over again, just trying to keep my sanity. Again I prayed the Lord's Prayer and then I went back to sleep.

There were two more nights to go before I was to fly out of Mauritius to New Zealand. The next night I was woken by a tapping on my window. It was a girl saying, "Ian, I want to talk to you, let me in." As I knew the girl I thought nothing of it. Half asleep I walked to the door and unlocked it. The moment I opened the door she grabbed it and I saw her eyes. I could see the same red tinge in her eyes that I had seen in the eyes that had haunted me for the last two nights. She began to speak in word perfect English. She was Creole and had never spoken perfect English. She said, "You are coming with us tonight Ian. We are going to take you somewhere." Then I heard other footsteps coming. I tried to pull the door closed but it was as if this girl had gained a supernatural strength and I couldn't move it. Then out of my heart came the words, "In Jesus' name – go!" She reeled backwards as if she had been punched in the chest. As I watched her recoil back up I slammed the door in her face and locked it. I was shaken but safe for the meantime.

Finally, it was my last night and I was all packed and ready to go. A taxi was coming for me at 5am. I went to sleep but was woken in the night, this time by stones hitting the window. It was the girl again. I was prepared and had locked the doors, but I had left a small window open. I thought, "Whatever these creatures are, they are out to kill me and they are using humans to do it!" I was about to jump up and shut the window when a big black arm came through it and flicked the latch. I heard the girl softly saying, "Ian, we want to talk to you. Come out." I was pretending to be asleep and the stones came on the windows again. This time she was louder, "Ian, come out." Then heavier stones began coming right through the window and she was angry now, "Ian, come out!"

I turned suddenly and saw a spear coming through the open window towards me. I grabbed my flashlight. "The best form of defence is attack" I thought, and I shone the flashlight into the spear wielder's eyes. There was that red tint again! I leapt up screaming for all I was worth, grabbed his spear and thrust it back at him so he loosed its hold. I threw it out the window and slammed the window shut. Quickly I shone the flashlight outside on three men and a woman. They cowered away like dogs about to be stoned. What amazed me was how afraid of the light they were.

I was so shaken that I stayed awake the rest of the night waiting for the taxi to come. But it never came. I woke my surfing friends and asked if they would go find the taxi for me. They found it debilitated. Someone had thrust steel rods through its radiator in the night. It was the only taxi in town and my friend had to go to the next town to get a taxi for me there. By the time he returned there were a group of Creole's outside my house with sticks and the driver was too afraid to drive past them. Apparently, I had caused quite a sensation in the town because of my miraculous recovery. The townsfolk knew I should have been dead and being a superstitious people, considered me a ghost or something worse. I managed to evade the antagonists though and made it to the airport to board my flight to New Zealand via Australia.

In Perth I caught up with my younger brother who was living there. I tried to tell him what I had seen. He was shocked and couldn't believe it. I slept in his room that night as he had left to return to New Zealand, and in the middle of the night I awoke to have white-eyed demons attacking me. I stormed out of the room to see sitting in the fireplace a small Buddha. As I looked at it God spoke to me that the white-eyed demons came out of this idol. I was amazed! Now I knew that what I had experienced with the idols in Colombo was demonic. I decided to shorten my trip to Australia and return to New Zealand immediately.

On the plane descending into Auckland, New Zealand, I asked the Lord, "What have I become?" I had my Walkman on with 'Men at Work' playing. A voice spoke over the sound of the Walkman and said, "Ian, you have become a reborn Christian." I took off my Walkman and looked around to make sure no person on the aeroplane had said it. Then I reached into my bag for my dark glasses. I put them on and in the relative seclusion that they provided I quietly freaked out. A Christian! Is that what I was? Who would want to be a Christian? It hadn't yet occurred to me that that was what I had become.

My parents picked me up from the airport. Back home, my mum had left my bedroom with its surf posters exactly as it had been two years ago. It was like walking into a time warp. I'd come home to a refuge. I went to sleep that night and was woken in the middle of the night by something shaking me. By now I knew how to get rid of the demons using the name of Jesus and the Lord's Prayer. They had to go, but what were they doing in my bedroom, in my house? I was furious! I got up and decided to give them a verbal lashing! So I went for it! I woke my parents up but I went for it! I sat down on my bed and said, "God – I'm sick of these things harassing me in the middle of the night. What must I do to get rid of them?" He replied, "Read the bible." I said, "Next you'll be asking me to go to church! I haven't got a bible!" "Your father has a bible – go and ask him for it."

So, I did. I started reading from the beginning, from the book of Genesis:

Since this experience in 1982 I've been following Jesus Christ as my Lord and Saviour. Initially I spent some time on my sister's dairy farm in New Zealand getting my life sorted out. Midway through 1983 I joined YWAM (Youth with a Mission) and sailed with them around the Pacific Islands telling the people there about God's love. Then I went back into South East Asia and ministered among the unreached tribal people of Malaysia. For three years I worked in the jungles of Sarawak and the mainland peninsular. During this time I met my wife Jane.

Since then, I have worked both in the church (I am now an ordained minister), and as an itinerant speaker, travelling to many nations around the world sharing this testimony. My wife Jane and I have three beautiful children, Lisa, Michael and Sarah. Our desire is to continue sharing the amazing good news of God's unconditional love and mercy, and his provision through Jesus' death on the cross for forgiveness of our sins, to everyone we meet.

End Notes:

i. Christy Wilson Beam: Piatkus 2015 ISBN 978-0-349-40892-7

ii. (Free Download) http://aglimpseofeternity.org/ians-testimony/english/ For full story see "Clinically Dead: I've seen Heaven and Hell: Jenny Sharkey – Gospel Media

Heaven

Peaceful, holy, radiant, pure:
Through jewelled gates on golden floor,
Where blissful scents of angel throngs,
Attend the air with children's songs.
Each sick, miscarried, blighted soul,
Runs blemish-free: complete and whole.
And with their laughter, sunshine rays,
Ascend on high as holy praise.
Unmeasured splendour, fit for Kings,
Now opens up through angel wings,
As vibrant flowers and vivid green,
Offset this brilliant, blinding scene.
Sparkling gems adorn the street,
While mansions rise where diamonds meet,
And beauty shines from every view,
Reflecting back its light on you.
Then, as you're called before the throne,
To meet the God your spirit's known,
No words depict nor book can share,
The awesome love that meets you there . . . . . .

Juliet Dawn

CHAPTER TWO

Heaven

"I can safely say, on the authority of all that is revealed in the Word of God, that any man or woman on this earth who is bored and turned off by worship is not ready for heaven"
A W Tozer 1897-1963

"From heaven you came, precious babe, entered our world your glory veiled" – Graham Kendrick **(i)**

HEAVEN: Greek Ουρανό Strong's: 3772. ούρανός (ouranos)

Chambers Dictionary of Beliefs and Religions **(ii)** suggests that in general, heaven is the dwelling place of God and the angels, and that in traditional Christianity the ultimate eternal destiny of the redeemed, there to reign with Christ in glory. The entry for 'heaven' goes on to say that in the Bible, *"and it is usually conceived of high above the earth. In modern theology, it goes on to say, the emphasis is more on the quality, transformation, or fulfilment of life, the fully revealed presence of God, and the perfection of the divine-human relationship, than on a place."*

I think that the Chambers definition is a good place to start our thinking about heaven and what the Bible reveals about heaven.

According to some people and the internet, 'heaven' is the world's most famous gay nightclub located in Charing Cross, London. Apparently, the management reserve the right to refuse admission to those deemed to be wearing unsafe footwear! Well, thank goodness, that is what heaven for Christian believers **IS NOT!**

Another thought this time from Christian theologian N T Wright who says this of heaven *"Jesus's resurrection is the beginning of God's new project not to snatch people away from earth to heaven but to colonize earth with the life of heaven. That, after all, is what the Lord's Prayer is about."* **(iii)**

The late Billy Graham, perhaps speaking for all born-again Christians, said "My home is in Heaven. I'm just traveling through this world". Jesus said, "If you want to be perfect, go, sell your possessions and give to the poor, and you will have treasure in heaven"'

A helpful and authoritative definition comes from Alexander Cruden's Concordance **(iv)** in which he wrote in 1839 *"the word (heaven) is used of the abode of the redeemed after death and the second resurrection. It is also used of God without whom there would be no heaven. It is sometimes used of the air, as in the phrase 'birds or fowls of heaven' and for the sky, wherein the sun, moon and stars are placed."* The fundamental importance of heaven in God's plan and in His revelation of the truth to us can be seen from the repeated use of heaven, both as a noun and an adjective in both Old and New Testaments. For example, heaven (noun) occurs 136 times. Hosts of heaven [16], 'In' heaven [87]; 'into' heaven [14]; to heaven or unto heaven [40]. The phrase 'under heaven' [19]; the adjective 'heavenly' [21] and 'heavens' [89]. The term 'in the heavens' occurs 15 times. The number of occurrences certainly is not far behind that of 'love', Jesus, and Salvation but certainly doesn't get near to God's divine name [6828]!!

There is, of course, an inherent danger in simply word counting and there is no substitute for reading the Bible, but that doesn't mean word-counting is worthless. In fact, real insight can come from the use of concordances, word studies, and even vocabulary lists, I don't know what I would do without them! It is also a theologian's tool. Bob Bell has many word-count tables in his book, 'The Theological Messages of the Old Testament' **(v)**, the culmination of many years of teaching Hebrew and Old Testament to students. He uses word-counting to help put on display themes or emphases in the text that he saw while reading. (source Mark Ward – Logos Talk "The Most Used Words in the Bible" **(vi)**)

Heaven or 'Paradise' is the term used to describe a place of timeless harmony, associated by Abrahamic faiths with the Garden of Eden. In Islam it is considered to be the final abode of the righteous (Jannah) and where believers are rewarded. The Arabic "Samawat" is also translated as heaven in the sense of the sky, sometimes referred to as the 'seven firmaments' or 'seven strong'. The seven layers of heaven are said to be analogous to the seven layers of hell (Jahannam). For Jihadi's it is where they are promised (by their leaders), the prize of seventy virgins for killing Jews and/or Christians. Thus for fundamental Islam, paradise is a place of unrestrained sexual activity where man can take advantage of women and girls . . . without restraint and responsibility . . . what righteous and loving God would decree and provide such nonsense? The Muslim heaven or paradise **IS NOT** the Biblical heaven.

Heaven, for born-again Christian believers, is the location of the throne of God and of his angels. The Insight Bible **(vii)** defines it as *"A place of perfect happiness and eternal communion with God"*. It is both a physical place and a temporary place where the righteous dead will live until the second coming of Christ. Heaven is also the dwelling place of God and all His people for eternity, described in scripture as the 'new heaven'. Hebrew thought and theology understood heaven in eschatological terms, that is, somewhere to be experienced immediately after death, yet to be experienced after the Great White throne Judgement and the coming of the new heaven and new earth. Heaven is also understood to be the 'waiting place', where believers go after the Rapture, and from where they return to the earth with Jesus at the Second Coming. On earth during the Millennium period believers will look forward to living in the New Heaven (Jerusalem) for eternity. The Christian writer and scholar David Pawson, who does not agree with this writer about a Pre-tribulation Rapture, also refers to heaven as 'only a waiting place'(viii).

Death is all around us today. People die from old age, illness, accidents, drugs, drink, negligence, wars and genocide. In the ancient world people lived with the reality of death and dead bodies. The dead had to be, and still are, buried quickly in hot climates. Grief and loss, confusion and anger were well known to the Israelites during their wilderness wanderings, their settlement in the Promised Land and their eventual exile and return. Yet death, however familiar to them, remained mysterious and frightening. It raised the obvious question of what happens to us after death? The Israelites called the dark and mysterious place of death "Sheol". They reasoned that when you go there, life seemed to be thoroughly finished. The Psalmists made it clear that they didn't want to go there and asked God what possible good there could be in death *"Are your wonders known in the place of darkness, or your righteous deeds in the land of oblivion?"* (Psalm 88:12)!

Death and Sheol meant for the Hebrews the end of their plans, worship and their relationship with God (Psalm 30:9; 88:5; 146:4). The dead were found there – not the living! Yet other Psalmists spoke about God's power over death (Psalm 139:8) and His power to redeem people from death (Psalm 49:7-9,15). And then came David's declaration that Jesus and God's people would not see decay, hallelujah! So, what would they and we see? The answer, again from the Psalms is that they would see God's face and His presence (Psalm 16:8-11; 17:15; 49:15 and 73:23-26). Paul's teaching in 2 Corinthians 5:1-10 is particularly revelatory and sits with the New Testament witness to life after death and the hope of eternal life. *"For we know that if the earthly tent we live in is destroyed, we have a building from God, an eternal house in heaven, not built by human hands. Meanwhile we groan, longing to be clothed instead with our heavenly dwelling, because when we are clothed, we will not be found naked. For while we are in this tent, we groan and are burdened, because we do not wish to be unclothed but to be clothed instead with our heavenly dwelling, so that what is mortal may be swallowed up by life. Now the one who has fashioned us for this very purpose is God, who has given us the Spirit as a deposit, guaranteeing what is to come. Therefore, we are always confident and know that as long as we are at home in the body we are away from the LORD. For we live by faith, not by sight. We are confident, I say, and would prefer to be away from the body and at home with the LORD. So, we make it our goal to please him, whether we are at home in the body or away from it. For we must all appear before the judgment seat of Christ, so that each of us may receive what is due us for the things done while in the body, whether good or bad"*. We do live by faith and this faith is aroused by confident declaration, despite what some would call controversial teaching!

In Psalm 16:10 (a miktam of David) we have the first definitive understanding of heaven as David declares *"because you will not abandon me to the grave (sheol) nor will you let your Holy One see decay"*. In this lovely, confident and happy psalm, King David rejoices that the life that God alone gives cannot be cancelled by the grave. Whilst the Old Testament carries hints of life after death, David, because of his relationship with God, has a deeper understanding that death is not the end for believers. St Paul understood this Psalm as prophesying the resurrection of Jesus (Acts 2:25-28 & 13:35-37). Furthermore, Paul knew that because of the resurrection of Jesus, David and all of God's people would be raised to new life in Jesus.

Having said all this, however, there is much more that the Scriptures teach us about heaven. Firstly, it is where God rules from (or from whence God rules). *"Heaven is My throne and the earth is My footstool"* says God (Isaiah 66:1-2) and where He reigns sitting between the cherubim (Psalm 99:1). Jesus taught the disciples that heaven is where our treasures are *"Do not store up for yourselves treasures on earth, where moths and vermin destroy, and where thieves break in and steal. But store up for yourselves treasures in heaven, where moths and vermin do not destroy, and where thieves do not break in and steal. For where your treasure is, there your heart will be also. The eye is the lamp of the body. If your eyes are healthy, your whole body will be full of light. But if your eyes are unhealthy, your whole body will be full of darkness. If then the light within you is darkness, how great is that darkness! No one can serve two masters. Either you will hate the one and love the other, or you will be devoted to the one and despise the other. You cannot serve both God and money"*. (Matthew 6:19-24). Later, during His final teaching on the Second Coming, Jesus makes it clear through His parable on the sheep and the goats that heaven is only for the righteous (Matthew 25:31-46). The Great White Throne Judgement (Revelation 20:11-15) ends with the unrighteous being thrown into the Lake of Fire and eternal punishment, whereas the righteous will enter eternal life. That is surely why Jesus teaches during the Sermon on the Mount that we must *"seek first the Kingdom of God and His righteousness"* (Matthew 6:33)

It would be wrong and dishonouring to God to think that that is all that Scripture tells us about Heaven. The Scripture is very clear that we will one day, through faith, inhabit something better than what had been promised, i.e. Heaven where we and all the saints of old will be perfected together (Hebrews 11:40). For the time being, in this life, we are 'Citizens of Heaven' (Philippians 3:12-4:1) but after the Great White Throne Judgement we will be for ever in the New Heaven.

It is vital, therefore, that we are not in ignorance about heaven. In 1 Thessalonians 4:13, the Apostle Paul writes *"Brothers and sisters, we do not want you to be uninformed about those who sleep in death, so that you do not grieve like the rest of mankind, who have no hope."* The expression "those who fall asleep" means those who have died. Those who have died in faith, says Paul, will be taken by Jesus to heaven. The Apostle goes on to then say that those who are alive when Jesus comes for the Church will be caught up with Him in the air and taken to heaven. The heaven that Paul is describing is not the heaven of eternal life but, is a 'waiting place' as we discussed earlier. In his book "Heaven" Randy Alcorn calls it the 'Present Heaven' **(viii)**. In other words, it is the place that Christians go to when they die, but it is also where Christ is. It is also where the angelic beings live but it is also a place with a past (the time prior to Christ's incarnation, death and resurrection), it has a present (the heaven where believers go when they die) and it has a future (the eternal heaven or New Earth).

It is therefore incorrect to think that the heaven that we go to at death is the same as the heaven where we spend eternity. There are major differences borne out in Scripture. For example, God doesn't dwell with those in the present heaven but only with those in the eternal heaven. This is because the New Heaven will be established on earth as will the New Jerusalem (Revelation 21:1-2). Once that happens then God will dwell with them and they will be His people. This emphasises another important difference, that of the incarnation. We celebrate the incarnation of God during our Christmas worship, thinking and preaching. We will once again celebrate the incarnation in the New Heaven, because God will dwell with His people. Another major difference concerns the realm of each heaven. Only a deep study of Scripture will reveal these things and we would be indebted to scholars like Randy Alcorn **(ix)**, Peter Toon **(x)** and Alistair

McGrath (**xi**) for revealing these to us. Put simply scripture shows that the present heaven is in the angelic realm whereas the future heaven will be in the earthly realm. The New Jerusalem which was in heaven, will come out of heaven and go to the New Earth and there the redeemed will spend eternity in their resurrection bodies, inhabiting heaven on the New Earth. God and Jesus will surely come and make their home with those who love Him (John 14:23). God will also, once more, walk among men (Genesis 3:8). Randy Alcorn makes the point that this is a picture of God's ultimate plan – not to take us up to live in a realm made for Him, but to come down and live with us in the realm He made for us!

All this, however, cannot take place until after the Great White Throne Judgement. Only then can the redeemed of the Lord live with him in sinless perfection and peace. Thus the New Heaven becomes fully compatible with the New Earth.

Scripture also gives us a glimpse of heaven in Revelation chapters 4-6. The glimpse starts with worship in heaven (Ch 4) then moves to the glory and holiness of the Lamb, who alone can break the seals (Ch 5). Chapter 6 gives a startling image of Jesus, the helpless Lamb who is also the mightiest of all. Everything then reaches a climax with the 144,000 witnesses; the vastness of heaven, its population (the Great Multitude), and eternal worship. The perfect plan of God is fulfilled, and His people are before Him enjoying the reality of God's eternal presence. *"Therefore, they are before the throne of God and serve Him day and night in His temple; and He who sits on the throne will shelter them with His presence. . . . For the Lamb at the centre of the throne will be their shepherd; 'he will lead them to springs of living water.' 'And God will wipe away every tear from their eyes.'* (Isaiah 25:8, 49:10 and also* Revelation 7:15-17).

End Notes:

i. **From Heaven You came** – Graham Kendrick: *Kingsway*
ii. **Chambers Dictionary of beliefs and Religion** – Mark Vernon: **ISBN-10**: 9780550103444
iii. **Surprised by Hope: Rethinking Heaven, the Resurrection, and the Mission of the Church** – N.T. Wright
iv. **Crudens Complete Concordance of the holy Bible** – Alexander Cruden: Lutterworth Press 2002 Edition.
v. **The Theological Messages of the Old Testament** – Bob Bell:
vi. **Most Used Words in the Bible** – Mark Ward:
vii. **The Insight Bible NIV Version**: Hodder & Stoughton
viii. **When Jesus Returns** – David Pawson: Hodder & Stoughton
ix. **Heaven** – Randy Alcorn: Tyndale
x. **Heaven and Hell - A Biblical and Theological Overview** – Peter Toon: Nashville: Nelson 1986
xi. **A Brief History of Heaven** – Alistair E McGrath: Malden: Mass: Blackwell 2003

Hell

Putrid, pungent, rancid, vile:
The belly of hell presents its bile.
Tormented cries and anguished moans,
Decaying flesh and blackened bones.
Insidious worms that stake their claim,
To what was once your living frame;
Fraying joints and sinew dregs,
Were once your earthly arms and legs.
Holes for eyes and claws for fists,
Your soul a swirling, dirty mist.
Mocking laughter, piecing spears;
Demonic sport, eternal years.
Constant burning, ceaseless pain,
That sends your knowing mind insane.
A stenchful home of brimstone pits;
Consuming flames in starts and fits.
Here memories of yesterlife,
Intersperse regret and strife,
And when all fragile hope has gone,
This endless hell, just stretches on . . . . . .

Juliet Dawn

CHAPTER THREE

Hell

Go to hell!
If you're going through hell, keep going.
Winston Churchill

Do not be afraid of those who kill the body but
cannot kill the soul. Rather, be afraid of the One
who can destroy both soul and body in hell.
Matthew 10:28 NIV

"The word 'hell' is probably the most
misunderstood word in the Bible" Roger Price **(i)**
HELL: *Greek Ηαδεσ = Hades: Hebrew =* שְׁאוֹל*=*
Sheol: Strongs 7585 **(ii)**

Let us begin our consideration of the facts about hell with these
three Biblically based statements: **Firstly,** everyone will exist
eternally either in heaven or hell. There are four key passages of
scripture that affirm this. These are Daniel 12:2-3 *"Multitudes*
who sleep in the dust of the earth will awake: some to everlasting
life, others to shame and everlasting contempt. ³Those who are
wise will shine like the brightness of the heavens, and those who
lead many to righteousness, like the stars for ever and ever".

This is followed by the parable of the sheep and the goats in Matthew 25:46 when Jesus ends the parable with these words: *"Then they will go away to eternal punishment, but the righteous to eternal life."* Jesus, when talking about himself and His right to give life told the Jews who were persecuting Him on the Sabbath, *"Do not be amazed at this, for a time is coming when all who are in their graves will hear his voice and come out— those who have done what is good will rise to live, and those who have done what is evil will rise to be condemned".* (John 5:28-29). Finally, we can turn to Revelation 20:14-15 to see what happens at the Final Judgement *"then death and Hades were thrown into the lake of fire. The lake of fire is the second death. Anyone whose name was not found written in the book of life was thrown into the lake of fire".* The **second** statement is that everyone has only one life in which to determine their destiny (Hebrews 9:27). **Thirdly,** the eternal destination of heaven or hell is determined by faith in Christ alone to save us. (John 3:16 and John 3:36).

Let us face it, hell is not a regular subject of after dinner conversation. It is a subject that most people see not to want to discuss. "Hell is the most offensive and least acceptable of all Christian doctrines" writes David Pawson. "We try to ignore it but it won't go away. We attempt to explain it away, but it keeps coming back. Better to face the truth, even if it hurts!" **(iii)**

The word hell is generally used in the Old Testament to translate the Hebrew word 'Sheol' (שְׁאוֹל) that really means 'the place of the dead' or the 'grave' (NKJV). (Genesis 37:35; 42:38; 1 Samuel 2:6, Job 14:13 and Isaiah 7:11). We should add to that other passages which convey the idea of punishment. In the New Testament two Greek words are both translated as 'hell'. These are 'Hades' which generally means the same as Sheol, for example in Acts 2:27; 1 Corinthians 15:55 and Revelation 20:13. The second word is 'Gehenna' which means the place of retribution for evil deeds. In Eastons

Bible Dictionary **(iv)** it is defined (originally Ge bene Hinnom; i.e., "the valley of the sons of Hinnom"), a deep, narrow glen to the south of Jerusalem, where the idolatrous Jews offered their children in sacrifice to Molech (2 Chronicles 28:3; 33:6; Jeremiah 7:31; 19:2-6). This valley afterwards became the common receptacle for all the refuse of the city. Here the dead bodies of animals and of criminals, and all kinds of filth, were cast and consumed by fire kept always burning. It thus in process of time became the image of the place of everlasting destruction. In this sense it is used by our Lord in Matthew 5:22 Matthew 5:29 Matthew 5:30; 10:28; 18:9; Matthew 23:15 Matthew 23:33; Mark 9:43 Mark 9:45 Mark 9:47; Luke 12:5. In these passages, and also in James 3:6, the word is uniformly rendered "hell," the Revised Version placing "Gehenna" in the margin.

Dr Wayne Grudem in Chapter 56 of his book 'Systematic Theology' **(v)** defines 'hell' like this: *"A place of eternal conscious punishment for the wicked (Luke 16:22-24; Revelation 14:9-11; 19:1-3; 20:10; Matthew. 25:41). Some (Christians) deny the existence of hell. One of the most common ways to deny this is through the doctrine of 'annihilationism'".*

Annihilationism: The view that after the wicked have suffered the penalty of God's wrath for a time, God will annihilate them so that they no longer exist. Arguments in favour of this view: 1. The biblical references to the destruction of the wicked implies that they will no longer exist after they are destroyed (Greek apōleia, Philippians 3:19 – but see Matthew 26:8; or else olethros, 2 Thessalonians. 1.9) Response: The words translated "destruction" do not necessarily imply a ceasing to exist or annihilation but can simply be ways of referring to the harmful and destructive effects of final judgment on unbelievers. 2. The inconsistency of eternal conscious punishment with the love of God. Response: The same difficulty in reconciling God's love with eternal punishment would seem to be present in reconciling God's love with the idea of divine punishment at all. 3. The injustice of the disproportion between sins committed in time and punishment that is eternal. Response: This wrongly assumes we know the extent of the evil done when sinners rebel against God. – Also, unbelievers in hell may go on sinning and receiving punishment for their sin, never repenting. 4. The continuing presence of evil creatures in God's universe will eternally mar the perfection of a universe that God created to reflect his glory. Response: When God punishes evil, the glory of his justice, righteousness, and power to triumph over all opposition will be seen. (Romans 9:22-24) "

The New Testament tells us that hell was originally intended for satan and his demons In Matthew 25:41 Jesus said, *"Then he will say to those on his left, 'Depart from me, you who are cursed, into the eternal fire prepared for the devil and his angels"*. John's Revelation tells us that at the Final Judgement *"And the devil, who deceived them, was thrown into the lake of burning sulphur, where the beast and the false prophet had been thrown. They will be tormented day and night for ever and ever"*. However, the New Testament also confirms that all the wicked dead will go to Hell (Revelation 20:10).

When Jesus told the parable about the Rich Man and Lazarus (Luke 16:22 – 30) He indicated that the Rich man went to hades [also referred to as an intermediate hell, in conscious torment – The AV translation has 'torments' (Luke 16:24)], but the righteous, in this case, the poor man, went to "Abraham's bosom" (Luke 16:22) also called 'paradise' (see Luke 23:43). After the Ascension of Christ according to Ephesians 4:8-10, paradise becomes 'the Third Heaven' which is separated from hell by a 'great gulf' (Luke 16:26 & 2 Corinthians 12:1-4) (for a fuller explanation see Ungers p531) **(vi)**. Hell will also in itself be an eternal punishment for those who reject Christ (Matthew 13:41-50 and Revelation 20:10). Hell is also quite clearly a place of conscious torment (Matthew 13:50; Mark 9:48 & Revelation 14:10). At the Final Judgment, the wicked dead are raised and cast into eternal hell, together with death and hades. This is referred to as the second death or eternal separation from God. In other words, it is the final state of the wicked. In Isaiah 66:24 the Lord warns that the destiny of the wicked is eternal perdition or Gehenna (see also Mark 9:44-48 and Rev 20:14-15). The NLT renders the Isaiah text like this *"and as they go out, they will see the dead bodies of those who have rebelled against me. For the worms that devour them will never die, and the fire that burns them will never go out. All who pass by will view them with utter horror."* This is such a graphic description and the utter horror of it is enough to cause us to shrink from sin. The Message Bible **(vii)** translates the same passage: *"And then they'll go out and look at what happened to those who rebelled against me. Corpses! Maggots endlessly eating away on them, an endless supply of fuel for fires. Everyone who sees what's happened and smells the stench retches."*

The Fate of False Teachers and child molesters

In his second letter, St Peter in writing to the Early Church warns what will happen to false teachers. He says, *"But there were also false prophets among the people, even as there will be false teachers among you, who will secretly bring in destructive heresies, even denying the Lord who bought them, and bring on themselves swift destruction. And many will follow their destructive ways, because of whom the way of truth will be blasphemed. By covetousness they will exploit you with deceptive words; for a long time, their judgment has not been idle, and their destruction does not slumber. For if God did not spare the angels who sinned but cast them down to hell and delivered them into chains of darkness, to be reserved for judgment"* (2 Peter 2:1-4). The Greek word for hell in verse 4 is Tartarus Tartarus – which means 'put in hell' (Greek New Testament Dictionary). It is not only false teachers who will be so punished by the wrath of God (2 Peter 2:1-3), but also those who cause children to sin. Jesus reserves a place too for the unrepentant child molester or for anyone who places a spiritual stumbling block in the way of children and young people. Surely this is sufficient warning for our immoral society and law-makers?

In Mark 9:42-43 NLT we read *"But if you cause one of these little ones who trusts in me to fall into sin, it would be better for you to be thrown into the sea with a large millstone hung around your neck. If your hand causes you to sin, cut it off. It's better to enter eternal life with only one hand than to go into the unquenchable fires of hell* (Gehenna)*with two hands"*. [where the maggots never die, and the fire never goes out! – Author]. In addition to these heretics and unrighteous sinners', 2 Peter 2:4 tells us that Tartarus is the place reserved for fallen angels where they will be judged.

Paradise was also part of hell and the waiting place of the Old Testament saints which became part of heaven when Jesus died on the cross. Jesus went to Paradise when he died and witnessed to hell that He had victory over death. He then led all the saints and even Paradise itself into heaven as part of His victory procession; Jesus then presented Himself to the Father as the first fruits sacrifice. No wonder the Apostle Paul writes *"But thanks be to God, who always leads us in triumphal procession in Christ and through us the fragrance of the knowledge of Him"* (2 Corinthians2:14) to which we should be responding in our spirit Halleluiah! Glory to God! St Paul himself experienced Paradise when he was stoned to death (Acts 14:19) and he confirmed this in his second letter to the Corinthians 12:4 where he "was caught up to Paradise".

A Diagrammatic representation of the stages of hell is as follows:

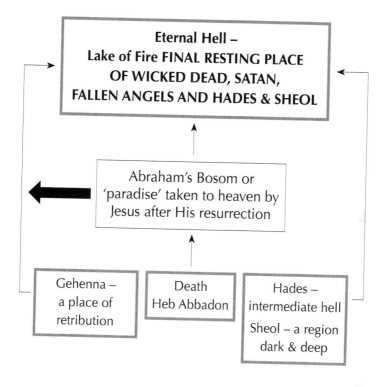

In Job 26:6 the Hebrew word Abaddon is used to describe hell, although it is translated in the NIV as "death". Similarly, in Isaiah 66:24 and Revelation 9:11 the Greek word Gehenna is used and translated as Abyss. *"They had as king over them the angel of the Abyss, whose name in Hebrew is Abaddon and in Greek is Apollyon (that is, Destroyer).* (Rev 9:11)

We might also represent Hell in all its forms as Underworld departments. A typical diagrammatic representation is as follows: – **(viii)**

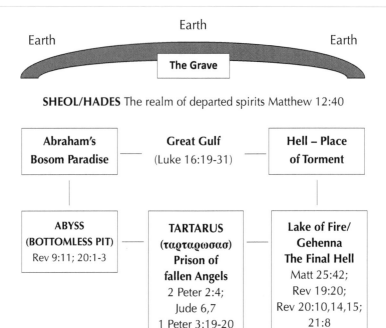

SHEOL/HADES The realm of departed spirits Matthew 12:40

Abraham's Bosom Paradise	Great Gulf (Luke 16:19-31)	Hell – Place of Torment

ABYSS (BOTTOMLESS PIT) Rev 9:11; 20:1-3	TARTARUS (ταρταρωσασ) Prison of fallen Angels 2 Peter 2:4; Jude 6,7 1 Peter 3:19-20	Lake of Fire/ Gehenna The Final Hell Matt 25:42; Rev 19:20; Rev 20:10,14,15; 21:8

What hell is not

One example comes from Rev Dr Rowan Williams, once the most senior cleric in the Established church, who said in 2009 on Channel 4 TV, when questioned about faith and God, said "I think I'd prefer to talk about being confident that God exists, or trusting that God exists. "It's not knowing as you know a state of affairs in the world, it's much more of a sense that you're in the presence of something greater than you can conceive. I suppose from my teens I have just been aware of that something greater than I can put words to in whose presence I live." But he admitted he has suffered "moments of strain in faith". **(viii)**

Asked by film maker Antony Thomas about what happens to the soul after death, the Archbishop replied: "All we really know about the after-life is that God has promised to be there." When asked if hell exists and what it is like, he said: "My concept of hell, I suppose, is being stuck with myself for ever and with no way out. Whether anybody ever gets to that point I have no idea. But that it's possible to be stuck with my selfish little ego for all eternity, that's what I would regard as hell." **(ix)** When told that this does not look sound like the Biblical image of the damned being tortured in lakes of fire beneath the earth, Dr Williams replied that being alone forever "is torment enough if you think about it!" Some people might like the idea of being alone, but such sentiments ignore or exclude the Biblical witness about the nature of hell as well as the Sovereignty of God, who alone judges the righteous and the unrighteous. Such thoughts also make the cross and the sacrificial death of Christ of no consequence, thus robbing the gospel of its power and truth!

A further example is found in a new book written by Craig Unger (New York Times Best Selling Author), entitled "House of Trump; House of Putin" **(x).** This followed his earlier political expose "House of Bush; House of Saud", Craig Unger's painstaking research into the Russian Mafia and its links with both Putin and Trump describes the violence, thuggery, illegality and control exercised by international Mafia bosses, particularly those in Putin's close circle of multi-millionaires, oligarchs and FSB officers. It also charts one of the greatest intelligence operations in history, ending with an American president apparently under the control of a Russian President. Craig Unger writes on p127, "In Moscow, of course, since the demise of the Soviet Union, the KGB has been replaced by the FSB, but that did not mean its vaunted tradecraft had been lost or in any way diminished. To the contrary, the Kremlin was now being run by a career KGB operative – in fact, one whose life's goal was to revive Russia's shattered dreams of empire. To that end, at almost every turn there is evidence of the Russians throwing the KGB textbook at Trump, trying to entangle him and compromise him in as many ways as possible. And in Trump, the Russians seemed to have found the perfect mark."

That statement is horrendous in its implications. The extent and brutality of these mafia groups seen in both Russia and America can only be described as hellish and the actions of the all-powerful Russian president pure evil. Reading some of the descriptions leaves one mentally and spiritually brutalized but it is not hell.

Hell is eternal death in the Lake of Fire suffering torment of the soul in the most frightening of environments. Hell is for the unbeliever and the unrepentant sinner.

The Authority of Jesus over all powers

The New Testament makes explicit that fact that Jesus has established through His death and resurrection, authority over all powers (Ephesians 1:20-23). This includes 'the one who holds the power of death' (Hebrews 2:14 and 2 Timothy 1:10). Paul triumphantly proclaims that Jesus is "Lord both of the living and of the dead" (Romans 14:9). As has already been noted earlier, Jesus has to enter Hades to proclaim His victory over death and deliver the Old Testament saints into heaven. Jesus himself prophesied that the *'Son of Man will be delivered from the heart of the earth just as God delivered Jonah from Hades (*Matthew 12:40). It is interesting that in the first century AD, Peter saw King David's prophecy in Psalm 16:10 *"because you will not abandon me to the realm of the dead, nor will you let your faithful one see decay"* as God delivering Jesus from Hades (See Acts 2:27 & 2:31).

In Baker's Evangelical Dictionary of Biblical Theology (**xi**), Timothy Phillips comments "However, Jesus' descent to Hades is theologically important. This is the path of the Old Testament righteous (Isaiah 53). Furthermore, this descent confirms that God assumed human nature and even our sinful destiny, death (2 Corinthians 5:14,21; Hebrews 2:14). Finally, Jesus' deliverance from Hades establishes the new life for humanity (1 Corinthians 15)". He goes on to conclude his commentary with this statement "The end of Hades: Jesus is the conqueror of all powers, the exalted One, and as such he has graced his church (see Ephesians 4:7-10). With Hades vanquished (Revelation 1:18) believers know that nothing, not even death, cannot separate them from Christ (Romans 8:39). They still await the next act in the history of salvation, when Jesus consummates his kingdom. Then Hades will release its dead for the final resurrection and judgment (Revelation 20:13). Thereafter Hades, Satan, and the reprobate will be thrown into Gehenna, the place of God's final retributive punishment. (Hades has only a limited existence; Gehenna or hell is the final place of judgment for the wicked. Many English versions foster confusion by translating both terms as "hell").

In summary, the New Testament affirms that Christ has conquered Hades. While dead believers exist in this state, they are also "with the Lord." Hades also denotes the vanquished stronghold of Satan's forces whose end is certain and the intermediate place of punishment for the wicked dead until the final judgment. Praise the Lord for His salvation and the hope of eternal life that we, as believers, have through Jesus.

End Notes:

i.   What happens After Death?: Roger price – Sovereign World International

ii.   **The New Strong's Expanded Exhaustive Concordance of the Bible**: James Strong – Thomas Nelson 2010

iii. **The Road to Hell**: David Pawson – Hodder & Stoughton

iv.   **Eastons Illustrated Bible Dictionary Third Edition**: Published by Thomas Nelson 1897

v.   **Systematic Theology**: Wayne Grudem – Zondervan

vi.   **Ungers Bible Handbook**: Moody Press Chicago 1967

vii. **The Message**: Eugene H Petersen – Navpress

viii. **The Five Underworld Departments** – courtesy of Roger French

ix.   Reported in the Telegraph 13th August 2009

x. **House of Trump House of Putin** – Craig Unger: Bantam Press 2018
xi. **Bakers Evangelical Dictionary of Biblical Theology.** Edited by Walter A Elwell – Baker Books 1996

CHAPTER FOUR

The development of heaven and hell cosmology

"Sometimes I think we're alone in the universe, and sometimes I think we're not. In either case, the idea is quite staggering." Arthur C. Clarke

"Something deeply hidden had to be behind things." Albert Einstein, Autobiographical Notes

"When I was a boy, the thought of heaven used to frighten me more than the thought of hell.....
I pictured heaven as a place where time would be perpetual Sundays with perpetual chapel services from which there would be no escape."
David Lloyd George 1863-1945

The Welsh Pastor, Paul Young, said in a talk on heaven "Satan wants us to have a distorted view of heaven" **(i)**. How right he is, hence, the need for this book and others like it. If we were to study Hebrew cosmology and its development through New Testament times and Greek thought up to the present day, we might find that most commentaries and Bible Dictionaries do not have much in the way of detailed material. To say "It's up there"; "It's the highest heaven" or even "the Third heaven" does not end the investigation into where and what is heaven. To understand by revelation and interpretation about heaven requires more work and thought. We will attempt to do this in this chapter.

Firstly, it seems to me that if we are to have a Biblical understanding of Heaven and Hell to support an evangelical faith and a Pre-Tribulation End Times view (see Chapter Six) then we could do with some more background knowledge to help us. It would be very easy to allow scriptural cosmology, particularly New Testament cosmology, to be made to suit both scientific and philosophical views. This chapter will hopefully lead us into a more Biblical and Evangelical picture from which we can make sense of texts dealing with or prophetically speaking about precisely where heaven and hell are.

Secondly, there may well be a predisposition towards one view of heaven that we all have according to our upbringing, Bible knowledge and spiritual experience. It may be stronger in some that others. Hell-fire and damnation preaching has clearly reached many in years gone by, irrespective of what cosmology was understood or believed. In our twenty first century cultural Marxist State, with its anti-Christ E.U. influence and One World agenda, we are experiencing powerful spiritual warfare (a precursor of the seven-year Great tribulation?). It seems to me more important that we must have an understanding and experience born of more rigorous study, in order that we can be firmly rooted in our faith and scripture.

We begin this study in the Old Testament. King Solomon dedicated the newly built temple with prayer. He stood before the altar of the Lord and stretched out his hands to heaven. His prayer in 1 Kings chapter eight contains examples of his cosmology. For example, in verse 23 he prays *"O Lord, God of Israel, there is no God like You in heaven above or on earth below . . ."* This is followed in verse 27 with the question *"But will God really dwell on earth? The heavens, even the highest heaven cannot contain You. How much less this temple I have built."* Moses under the leading of the Spirit saw another view of heaven. In Deuteronomy 26:15, he praises God with these words," Look *down from heaven, your holy dwelling place, and bless your people Israel and the land you have given us as you promised on oath to our ancestors, a land flowing with milk and honey."* Moses also tells us that Jacob received Isaac's blessing and went in obedience to Isaac's command to find a wife. On his way to Haran from Beersheba he lay down to sleep and had a dream. Moses recorded in Genesis 28:12-13 that Jacob *"had a dream in which he saw a stairway resting on the earth, with its top reaching to heaven, and the angels of God were ascending and descending on it. There above it stood the LORD, and He said: 'I am the LORD, the God of your father Abraham and the God of Isaac. I will give you and your descendants the land on which you are lying'".*

Clearly, the stairway was certainly not a ladder, but a solid and stable structure able to accommodate the angels of God ascending and descending on it. The sign of the ladder was clearly from God and indicated that He would be Jacob's God. At the top of the stairway stood God, how awesome! God was in heaven and heaven is above the earth. God resides in heaven and that is where His throne is (Isaiah 66:1 *This is what the LORD says: "Heaven is my throne, and the earth is my footstool. Where is the house you will build for me? Where will my resting place be?"*). At this point we have no further scientific detail but are left again with the cosmological question of where and how heaven fits into creation and its relationship to earth. Scripture does however provide more detail about heaven in so far as it is clearly not just the dwelling place of God but also of those closely associated with Him. Heaven we are told is where the faithful will dwell with God (Psalm 101:6) in safety (Leviticus 25:18) and together in unity (Psalm 133:1). It is also a place that is reserved for all the saved who have been born-again and is therefore our ultimate destination *"and into an inheritance that can never perish, spoil or fade. This inheritance is kept in heaven for you"* (1 Peter1:4).

The question that needs to be answered is that of where and what is heaven. This question is important particularly if heaven is what we are saved for and if it is our inheritance, where we will reside with God for eternity. Let us consider, therefore, the development of heaven cosmology. We will look at this beginning with medieval cosmology and then moving on to Judeo-Christian cosmology. We start with Dante's Cosmology. The University of Oregon cosmology website **(ii)** *reviews the development of cosmology from ancient thinking through the Middle Ages and then considers Copernicus and his influence on catholic theological thinking about heaven and hell.*

Dante's medieval Cosmology

From what we know it appears that the Catholic Church adopted most of Aristotle's worldview into early Christian thought, but Aristotle's finite Universe was at odds with the Church's idea of God's infinite power. Thus, the Church proposed an unlimited Universe rather than an infinite Universe, a subtle difference. A heliocentric Universe was impossible for the Church to adopt because it placed the sun at the centre of the universe rather than the earth. In the end medieval cosmology centred itself on the balance between the angelic sphere and the earthy realm. One such cosmology is found in Dante's `The Divine Comedy' which is an epic poem dealing with an allegorical vision of the afterlife and Catholic world-view. (Dante Alighieri [Dante]) was a major Italian poet of the late Middle Ages who died in September 1321). Dante's cosmology is illustrated by the following picture **(iii)**

Dante's cosmology is divided into three sections, firstly, theological doctrine, secondly, Inferno (Hell), Purgatory and thirdly, Paradise. The physical layout is such that Lucifer defines the very centre of the Universe and God is found in the outer region. Inside the Earth is found Hell, divided into nine circles for increasing levels of sin. Between the surface of the Earth and sphere of the Moon lies Purgatory (a mountain divided into seven terraces, displaced from the Earth when Lucifer's fall created Hell). Above Purgatory lies the spheres of Heaven, each describing a deficiency in one of the cardinal virtues. This model is not only over complicated, but it is also wrong. Lucifer, or the devil as he is also known, is not at the centre of the universe and, although there are five Greek verbs translated as 'sin', our sin (all of it, and whatever it was) is forgiven through the atoning blood of Christ as we repent and accept Jesus as our Lord and Saviour. I have struggled sometimes with C S Lewis' writing finding it as complicated as Dante's cosmology. Take this quote from his book "The Weight of Glory" in which Lewis writes *"At present we are on the outside of the world, the wrong side of the door. We discern the freshness and purity of morning, but they do not make us fresh and pure. We cannot mingle with the splendours we see. But all the leaves of the New Testament are rustling with the rumour that it will not always be so. Someday, God willing, we shall get in."* **(iv)**

The academics tell us that "despite the focus on religious concepts in the 'Divine Comedy', a great deal of its physical cosmology merges religious doctrine of the time into the Ptolemaic system (Claudius Ptolemy was a Greco-Roman mathematician, astronomer, astrologer and poet. He died in 1600AD). Philosophical and religious commentators say that the Ptolemaic system with various scientific additions parallels the discoveries from the time of Aristotle. For example, there are numerous references to a spherical Earth and changing constellations with latitude and varying time zones. The connection between the supernatural and the physical in Dante's cosmology mimics the Platonic viewpoint of the physical world being a copy of the world of Forms. Here the planetary spheres copy the angelic hierarchies that rotate around God (and the circles of Hell are a parody that rotates around Satan). Even the geocentric Universe (i.e. viewed from earth) is simply an imperfect copy of the spiritual form of Paradise, a theocentric Universe where the angels that power the motion of the planets are revolving around God, who illuminates all things from the centre. With perfect symmetry in both physical and theological space, Dante's cosmology represents the peak in medieval cosmology blending the Ptolemaic system with Christian doctrine".

The political and intellectual authority of the medieval church declined with time, leading, we are told, to the 'creative anarchy' of the Renaissance. This produced a scientific and philosophical revolution including the birth of modern physics.

Circles of Hell in Dante's Inferno

1st Circle: Limbo	The unbaptized and virtuous pagans including Virgil, Homer, Horace, Ovid, Socrates, Plato, and Saladin
2nd Circle: Lust	Souls are blown about in a violent storm, without hope of rest. Francesca da Rimini and her lover Paolo are here.
3rd Circle: Gluttony	The gluttons are forced to lie in vile, freezing slush, guarded by Ceberus. Ciacco of Florence is here.
4th Circle: Avarice & Prodigality	The Miserly and spendthrift push great heavy weights together, crashing them time and time again. Plutus guards them.
5th Circle: Wrath & Sullenness	The wrathful fight eachother on the surface of the Styx while the sullen gurgle beneath it. Filippo Argenti is here.
6th Circle: Heresy	Heretics are trapped in flaming tombs. Florentines Farinata degli Uberti and Cavalcante de' Cavalcanti are here.
7th Circle: Violence	The violent against people and property, the suicides, the blashphemers, the sodomites and the usurers.
8th Circle: Fraud	Panderes and seducers, flatterers, sorcerers and false prophets, liars, thieves, and Ulysses and Diomedes.
9th Circle: Treachery	Betrayers of special relationships are frozen in a lake of ice. Satan, Judas, Brutus, and Cassius are here.

© Wikipedia

Foremost to this new style of thinking was a strong connection between ideas and facts called the Scientific Method.

Since cosmology involves observations of objects very far away (therefore, very faint) advancement in our understanding of the cosmos has been very slow due to limits in our technology. This has changed dramatically in the last few years with the construction of large telescopes and the launch of space-based observatories (Galileo is credited with having developed **telescopes** for astronomical observation in 1609).

As we know from history, the great library at Alexandria burned down in 272 AD, destroying a great deal of the astronomical data for the time. Roman culture collapsed and the Dark Ages or Middle Ages as they were also known, began. The Dark Ages is a term given to describe the period in Britain after the Romans left in 476 AD up to the time of King

Alfred (849-901AD). During this time the Roman Catholic Church absorbed Aristotle's scientific methods and Ptolemy's model into its own doctrine. Thus, the scientific method and Ptolemy's Solar System were preserved. Unfortunately, the geocentric model was accepted as doctrine and, therefore, was not subjected to the scientific method for hundreds of years.

The period between the fall of the Roman Empire and the start of Renaissance in the 14th century was considered a time of scientific stagnation due to the recurring political and social upheavals of the time. The 14th century in Europe has often been called the 'Calamitous Century' and rightly so. The primary disruption of that century was obviously the appearance of the Black Death that was ultimately responsible for the gruesome death of more than 25 million people. Perhaps Europe was over-populated in at the start of the 14th century with simply too many mouths to feed. The 14th century was not an age of plenty. Add to this the peasant revolts in France and legal changes like the Statute of labourers which caused the English Peasants War in 1381. The decline in populations and inflation deeply disturbed 14th century Europe. The previous two or three centuries had been remarkably stable on the part of the labouring classes but the 14th century began to witness numerous peasant and urban revolts against the oppression of the propertied classes. This was something completely new and developed from a local circumstance made worse by famine and the plague.

There is now historical and archaeological evidence of thriving Christian communities throughout east and northern England during this time as the population grew and the beginnings of a nations could be seen. Major international trade grew during this period from places like Tintagel in Cornwall and business and cultural growth took place alongside the expansion of the Church. At the same time there was a continued steady progress in intellectual thought in Europe and surrounding kingdoms in the Middle East and India. While the

Catholic Church dominated most knowledge enterprises during this era, their influence was not as controlling as some would portray and various Church institutions were mostly responsible for the preservation of cosmological ideas from the Greeks. The distinction between what makes up matter (the primary elements) and its form became a medieval Christian preoccupation, with the sinfulness of the material world opposed to the holiness of the heavenly realm (which is interesting since modern cosmology is heavily consumed with the issue of dark matter exemplified to some extent at CERN). The medieval Christian cosmology placed the heavens in a realm of perfection, derived from Plato's Theory of Forms. The theory of Forms or theory of Ideas is a viewpoint attributed to Plato, which holds that non-physical forms represent the most accurate reality. When used in this sense, the word form or idea is often capitalized. Plato speaks of these entities only through the characters of his dialogues who sometimes suggest that these Forms are the only objects of study that can provide knowledge. The theory itself is contested from within Plato's dialogues, and it is a general point of controversy in philosophy. Even whether the theory represents Plato's own views is held in doubt by modern scholarship. However, the theory is considered a classical solution to the problem of universals). Source Wikipedia **(v)**

Pre-Copernican Cosmology

Cosmological thinking now begins to move forward as Nicolaus Copernicus (1500's) reinvented the heliocentric theory and challenged Church doctrine. Copernicus (d. 1543) was not the first astronomer to challenge the geocentric model of Ptolemy, but he was the first to successfully formulate a heliocentric model and publish his model. He placed the sun rather than the earth at the centre of the universe and was able to overcome centuries of resistance to the heliocentric model for a series of political and scientific reasons. Politically, the authority of the

Church was weakening in Northern Europe in the 15th century allowing more diversity in scientific thinking (although the new Protestant faiths were also not quick to embrace the heliocentric model). However, Copernicus, like Ptolemy, also used circular orbits and had to resort to epicycles and 'deferents' to explain retrograde motions. In fact, Copernicus was forced to use more epicycles than Ptolemy, i.e. a more complicated system of circles on circles. Thus, Copernicus' model would have failed our modern criteria that a scientific model be as simple as possible (i.e. using Occam's Razor which is a principle attributed to the 14th century logician and Franciscan Friar William of Ockham. Ockham was the village in the English county of Surrey where he was born. The principle states that "Entities should not be multiplied unnecessarily").

Ben Dupre says, 'Occam's Razor in essence is an injunction not to seek a more complicated explanation for something where a simple one is available' **(vi)**

JUDEO CHRISTIAN COSMOLOGY

Religious cosmology began with the ancient Hebrews and was developed from Old Testament texts. Later scrutiny has raised many questions and some contradictions. In my research I have been greatly helped by an online article produced by the University of Idaho **(vii).** The main facts and observations are taken from N. F. Gier, *God, Reason, and the Evangelicals* **(viii)**

In the diagram that follows (Ancient Cosmology), the area above the "ocean of heaven" is labelled the "heaven of fire" although this has not been verified. Again, various levels of heaven are not unique to the Hebrews for we can read that other religions conceived of at least "three superior realms of heaven". One psalmist clearly distinguishes between the two levels: *"You highest heavens, and you waters above the heavens"* (Psalm 148:4). This area is exclusively Yahweh's domain: *"The heaven of heavens belongs to Yahweh ..."* (Psalm 115:16, AB); *"To the Lord your God belong heaven and the heaven of heavens . . ."* (Deuteronomy. 10: l4); and *"heaven and highest heaven cannot contain thee"* (1 Kings. 8:27). These passages have led to endless speculation about the various levels of heaven.

The firmament as the dome of heaven

The most striking feature of the Old Testament world is the "firmament," a solid dome

which separates "the waters from the waters" (Gen. 1:6). The Hebrew word translated in the Latin Vulgate as *firmamentum* is *raqia'* whose verb form means "to spread, stamp or beat out." The material beaten out is not directly specified, but both biblical and extrabiblical evidence suggests that it is metal. The word "firmament" is used to translate rāqîaʿ (רְקִיעַ), a word used in Biblical Hebrew. It is derived from the root raqqəʿ (רְקַע), meaning beat or spread out thinly", e.g., the process of making a dish by hammering thin a lump of metal . . . (Wikipedia). Early Church history records that this was the view of leading Church fathers like Theophilus of Antioch, Clement of Alexandria and Augustine of Hippo to name but a few. In 1554 John Calvin wanted to set aside the Biblical testimony about 'firmament' and go with the science of the day. He advised that firmament be referred to as 'clouds'. Other passages in the Old Testament that also use Biblical Hebrew term raqqa' include Psalm 19:1; Ezekiel 1:22 and Daniel 12:3. There is disagreement about the correct interpretation from theologians such as Henry Morris (The Genesis Record) and Merrill F Unger (Unger's Bible Handbook).

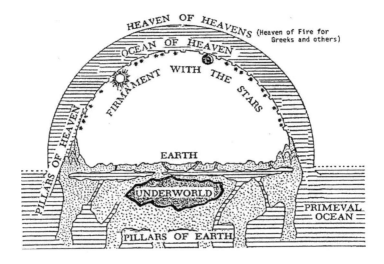

The idea of the dome or vault of heaven is found in many Old Testament books, e.g., *"God founds his vault upon the earth . . ."* (Amos 9:6). The Hebrew word translated as "vault" is *'aguddah'* whose verb form means to "bind, fit, or construct." Translations such as English Standard Version, The Berean Bible, and the New American Study Bible follow this translation but others like the NIV, KJV and New Living Bible do not. A somewhat less clear scripture supporting the understanding of 'dome' is found in Psalm 77:18 (Anchor Bible translation), the Hebrew בַּגַּלְגַּל (bag·gal·gal) according to Strong's Hebrew 1534: means A wheel, a whirlwind, dust. Whilst RSV translators translate *galgal* as "whirlwind," some argue that *galgal* is closely related to the Hebrew *gullath* (bowl) and *gulgolet* (skull), from which comes the idea of "something domed or vaulted." Perhaps this example illustrates the difficulty of settling on a fixed cosmology. As with any Biblical study research and wider reading from a variety of sources in needed.

Consequently, we must be careful not to impose our modern cosmology on the Hebrew world-view. An example is the Hebrew word חוּג (ḥūḡ) translated as spherical earth found in three references (Isaiah 40:22; Job 22:14; Proverbs 8:27). The Hebrew word *hug* used here cannot be translated as sphere (which is rendered by a different word כַּדּוּר) but may best be interpreted as a solid vault overarching the earth. The NIV has 'canopy', the NLT, NKJ and other modern translations have 'curtain' and 'tent'.

Therefore, the Anchor Bible translation of Isaiah 40:22: *"God sits upon the dome of the earth"* is much more accurate. Job 22:14 (NLT) says that God *"walks on the vault (hug) of heaven,"* again suggesting something solid. *Hug* can also refer to the circular perimeter of the sky-dome: *"He drew a circle (hug) on the face of the deep . . . and made firm the skies above"* (Proverbs. 8:27-28).

The second and most conclusive reason for taking the Hebrew solid heaven literally is that such a view was all over the ancient world of the time.

The final evidence I draw from rabbinic accounts. The ancient rabbis said: *"The heavens were in a fluid form on the first day, and on the second day they solidified."* Another ancient rabbi said: *"Let the firmament become like a plate, just as you say in Exodus 39:3."*

The pillars of heaven and earth

If we disengage ourselves from our own world-view, we can appreciate the internal logic of the Hebrew cosmology. If we are threatened by watery chaos from all sides, then a solid sky would be needed to hold back these ominous seas. If the sky is a solid dome, then it will need pillars to support it. Furthermore, if the earth is a flat disc floating on "the deep," then it would make sense for it to have some support to hold it in place.

It is not surprising then that one finds biblical references to the "pillars" or "foundations" of the heaven and earth. In Job we find that *"the pillars of heaven tremble, are astounded at God's rebuke"* (Job 26:11). In 2 Samuel we also find that God's anger makes *"the foundations of the heavens tremble"* (2 Samuel 22:8). God's fury also affects the pillars of the earth: *"Who shakes the earth out of its place, and its pillars tremble?"* (Job 9:6); and *"the foundations of the world were laid bare at thy rebuke, O Lord, at the blast of the breath of thy nostrils"* (Psalm 18:15). There seems to be a little confusion about where the pillars of heaven are located. Generally, it is agreed that in the Bible and other ancient literatures, distant mountains were the most likely candidates. But in one passage at least we find that Yahweh has *"laid the beams of his heavenly chambers on the waters"* (Psalm 104:3), i.e., the watery chaos surrounding the flat disc of the earth.

In the Old Testament God is portrayed as a cosmic architect. Isaiah asks: *"Who has measured the waters in the hollow of his hand and marked off the heavens with a span?"* (Isaiah 40:12). In Proverbs Yahweh *"drew a circle on the face of the deep . . . and marked out the foundations of the earth . . ."* (Proverbs 8:27-29). God challenges Job with the famous question: *"Where were you when I laid the foundations of the earth? . . .*

Who determined its measurements . . . or who stretched the line upon it? On what were its bases sunk, or who laid its cornerstone . . ." (Job 38:4). Continuing the same theme, the psalmists ask: *"Who placed the earth upon its foundations lest it should ever quake?"* (Psalm 104:5, Amplified Bible); and observe that *"when the earth totters . . . it is God who will steady its pillars"* (Psalm 75:3, Amplified Bible). Finally, in 1 Samuel 2:8 we find that *"the pillars of the earth are the Lord's and on them he has set the world."*

The waters above and below
In Genesis 1:1 we find the linguistic equivalent of Tiamat in the Hebrew word *tehom* ("the deep"), and the threat of watery chaos is ever present in the Old Testament. Evangelical Bible Commentator F. F. Bruce agrees that *"tehom* is probably cognate with Tiamat," and the American scholar Clark Pinnock admits that Yahweh also *"quite plainly . . . fought with a sea monster"*. The psalmists describe it in graphic terms: *"By thy power thou didst cleave the sea-monster in two and broke the dragon's heads above the waters; thou didst crush the many-headed Leviathan and threw him to the sharks for food"* (Psalm. 74:13-14 New English Bible; cf. Job 3:8; Isaiah. 27:1).

"The firmament separates the waters from the waters, so that there is water above the heavens and water below the earth" (Psalm l48:4). The Second Commandment makes this clear: *"You shall not make for yourself a graven image, or any likeness of anything that is in heaven above, or that is on the earth beneath, or that is in the water under the earth . . ."* (Deuteronomy 5:8; cf. Exodus 20:4; Isaiah 51:6). The lower tier of this three-storey universe is identified as water in other passages: *"God spread out the earth upon the waters"* (Psalm 136:6); and *"he has founded it upon the seas and established it upon the rivers"* (Psalm 24:2).

Although it sounds odd at first, the rabbinic idea that the sky-dome was made of congealed water makes eminent sense in terms of creation out of watery chaos. This doctrine, and not *creatio ex nihilo*, (ie 'out of nothing') is the prima facie implication of Genesis 1:1; and the scholarly consensus is that this initial impression is indeed correct. *"Ages ago I Sophia (wisdom) was set up . . . before the beginning of the earth. When there were no depths (tehom) I was brought forth . . ."* (Proverbs 8:23-24). Here there seems to be a clean break with previous creation models: watery chaos is not a coeternal substance along with Yahweh and Sophia, his co-craftsperson.

Celestial chambers and the heaven of heavens

While it is true that the Hebrews had a rough understanding of the circulation of water vapor and the source of rain in the clouds (Job 36:27, 28), they also conceived of mechanisms in heaven whereby God could directly induce great atmospheric catastrophes. Obviously, the clouds themselves could not have held enough water for the Great Flood, so *"all the foundations of the great deep burst forth, and the windows of the heavens were opened"* (Genesis 7:11; cf. Malachi 3:10). This is also further proof that the earth was surrounded by watery chaos. The Old Testament talks about divine "chambers" (*heder*) in heaven and this notion seems to have been borrowed from Canaanite mythology.

Significantly, we find that Yahweh *"brings forth the wind from his storehouses"* (Psalm 135:7); and *"from the chamber comes the tempest, from the scatter-winds the cold"* (Job 37:9, Amplified Bible). From Amos we learn that God *"builds his upper chambers in the heavens"* (Amos 9:6), and the psalmists speak of God storing "his upper chambers" with water so that he can water the mountains (Psalm 104:3, 13; cf. Psalm 33:7). Job gives us the most detailed account of God's chambers: *"Have you entered the storehouses of the snow, or have you seen the storehouses of the hail, which I have reserved for the time of trouble, for the day of battle and war?"* (Job 38:22).

We must not forget that *"Yahweh is a warrior"* (Exodus 15:3) and it is he, for example, who caused the violent storm which destroyed the Canaanite army of Sisera (Judges 5).

Hebrew Cosmology

If we place together all the Biblical arguments for the cosmology of the universe, we begin to see a picture emerging that is more faithful to the Hebrew texts and which helps us to then understand the cosmology of both heaven and earth. The following diagram illustrates ancient Hebrew cosmology.

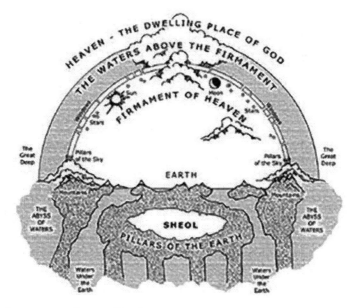

Source: www.funnygolfbooks.com

End Notes:

i.   Paul Young: Heaven – cd recording
ii. Abyss.uoregon.edu/~js/ast123/lectures/lec02.html
iii. Dantes Cosmology & Dantes model; Ancient cosmology taken from www:bing.com/images

iv. The Weight of Glory: C S Lewis
v. https://en.wikipedia.org/wiki/Theory_of_Forms
vi. 50 Philosophical ideas you really need to know – Ben Dupre: Quereus
vii. www.webpages.uidaho.edu/ngier/gre13.htm).
viii. (University Press of America, 1987), chapter 13. The Copyright is held by author whose copyright of the website article is acknowledged here.

CHAPTER FIVE

Bible cosmology of heaven and hell

"I sent my Soul through the Invisible,
Some letter of that After-life to spell:
And by and by my Soul return'd to me,
And answer'd: 'I Myself am Heav'n and Hell"
Omar Khayyam
https://www.goodreads.com/quotes/tag/heaven-and-hel/

"When we die, it's not the angels in heaven that
need our help. It's the angels in hell."
Anthony T. Hincks
https://www.goodreads.com/quotes/tag/heaven-and-hell

Aim at heaven and you will get earth thrown in.
Aim at earth and you get neither. **C S Lewis**

Introduction

Biblical cosmology is the biblical writers' conception of the cosmos as an organised, structured entity, including its origin, order, meaning and destiny. The sixty-six books of the Bible were written over many centuries, involving many authors and contributors about 40 in total although only 35 are positively identified **(i),** and reflected changing patterns of religious understanding and belief; consequently, its **cosmology** is not always consistent **(ii)**

Bible cosmology does not appear to be consistent because it has been a developmental science, in so far as the Biblical texts have been subjected to philosophical and scientific scrutiny over centuries and critiqued, while at the same time both philosophy and science in themselves have been developed and critiqued. Biblical interpretation has been a controversial science, undergoing many changes of methodology as differing schools of theology have put forward their own interpretations. German Biblical criticism is a good example. The Higher Criticism in this connection refers to a group of **German biblical** scholars centred in Tübingen, Germany, including Friedrich Schleiermacher (1768-1834), David Friedrich Strauss (1808-74) and Ludwig Feuerbach (1804-72),

In chapter three we have seen how early thought and understanding began to shape the emerging science of cosmology. Many of the models proposed were naïve but were the best that man could produce at the time. The other problem in coming up with a theory concerns the philosophical problem of how we see things and where we see them from. Plato advanced the idea of a cave (Plato's cave) in Book 7 of *The Republic* (375BC) Plato developed a parable of the cave in which he tried to show that there was one view from within the cave and another quite different one from outside. C S Lewis in his Chronicle of Narnia, seemed to use this method as when, in The Last Battle, the children enter Aslan's land, they realise that they have died and passed from the 'Shadowlands', a pale imitation of the beautiful and everlasting world that they now inhabit.

In the Seventeenth century John Locke (1690), an English philosopher, suggested that we only observe the outside world through a 'closet, wholly shut from light'. This theory had many holes in it, just as the closet had, to give light! But this theory known also as 'representative realism' still is highly influential today. From Locke, philosophy moved to Rene Descartes (1637) – the father of modern philosophy – who in his *Discourse on the Method* is looking for some firm foothold to help him as he feels stripped of every belief. He falls back on his own Cognito, hence the famous phrase "I think therefore I am" better translated "I am Thinking, therefore I am". This left him unable to prove the existence of heaven and hell because they were outside his cognisance.

The Biblical interpretation thus became challenged by philosophical thinking and theories, and none more so than David Hume (1748) the Scottish Philosopher, who said "....... *to have recourse to the veracity of the supreme Being, in order to prove the veracity of our senses, is surely making a very unexpected circuit.*" Hume also decried biblical miracles by saying that as we cannot define 'natural' then we cannot define 'supernatural'! All this leads us neatly to the crux of modern western philosophy, ie "Reason and Experience" and the Enlightenment.

Therefore, we press for an understanding of heaven and hell cosmology which is Biblically based, and which is textually accurate, and which makes sense. As we clearly cannot base our cosmology primarily on experience, we must take it by faith (Hebrews 11:1)

We begin by reminding ourselves of the ancient Hebrew conception of the Universe, shown by the following diagram and that in Chapter Three.

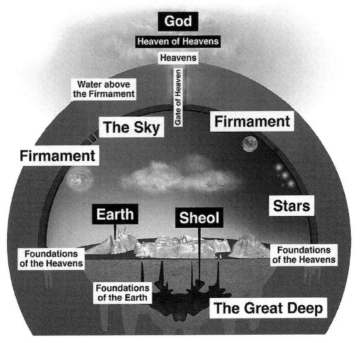

Ancient Hebrew Conception of the Universe

COPYRIGHT 2012 FAITHLIFE / LOGOS BIBLE SOFTWARE

Christian Cosmology

The Bible teaches a division of creation into invisible and visible – the heaven and the earth. For the bible, the unseen realm is intimately linked to the seen. Heaven is the counterpart to earth in a way analogous to the unseen Father's nature and character seen in His visible Image, Jesus. The Nicene Creed (325AD) puts it this way "Almighty God, Creator of all this is seen and unseen . . ." (However, these seen and unseen realms are reconciled to one another in the decisive, once-for-all event of the crucifixion . . ." *and through him to reconcile to himself all things, whether things on earth or things in heaven, by making peace through his blood, shed on the cross.* (Colossians 1:20)). There is no room in a Christian cosmology for multiple incarnations or multiple atonements. Christ does not bridge multiple universes in multiple incarnation, He bridges heaven and earth in His singular incarnation, hallelujah!

The development of Christian cosmology follows from the Hebrew understanding but refined by the New Testament. There appear to be three separate and distinct phases of this development. Ancient (400BC – 1600AD) Modern (1600 – 1950) and Post-modern (1950-Present). In the modern phase, philosophy thought begins to challenge earlier concepts of heaven and hell. Take this statement by Karl Barth (1886 – 1968) who was a Swiss Reformed theologian and is often regarded as the greatest Protestant theologian of the twentieth century **(iii)**

". . . *heaven and earth are related like God and man in the covenant, so that even the existence of creation is a single, mighty sign of the will of God. The meeting and togetherness of above and below, of the conceivable and the inconceivable, of the infinite and the limited – we are speaking of creation. All that is the world. But since within this world there really exist an above and a below confronting one another, since in every breath we take, in every one of our thoughts, in every great and petty experience of our human lives heaven and earth are side by side, greeting each other, attracting and repelling each other and yet belonging to one another, we are, in our existence, of which God is the Creator, a sign and indication, a promise of what ought to happen in creation and to creation – the meeting, the togetherness, the fellowship and, in Jesus Christ, the oneness of Creator and creature."* In his commentary on the Apostles' Creed, Barth observes that there is no mention of Satan, Hell or Eternal Death in the Apostles'

Creed, there is only mention of Eternal Life. And although this creed mentions Judgement, Barth says, it is not a Judgement into Eternal Hell, but to a restoration of justice. As a result of this subtle change of theological understanding, part of the Christian church rejects punishment, justice and a literal hell in favour of God's love shown supremely in relationship with his children, which relationship can be defined as 'heaven'. Most evangelical Protestant Christians would not accept this, insisting upon the witness of Scripture to the physical places of heaven and hell, for the believer and the unbeliever.

Augustine on Heaven and Rewards

We can benefit from Augustine's pastoral theology through the priority he places on the Christian's good works and their relation to heaven and heaven's rewards. What a human being does in response to God's grace *really matters* to Augustine – in fact, **it is a matter of heaven and hell** (bold type mine). Since the drama of salvation is a process finalized only at death, our moral choices throughout our life are not mere icing on the cake of an already finished state, but truly significant in the successful completion of our journey to salvation.

Even though Jesus often speaks of rewards as one way of motivating His followers, many of us become uneasy with such thinking. But at the end of the ages, Jesus will say one of two things to every person – either, "Depart from Me, for I never knew you," (Matthew 7:23) or, "Well done, My good and faithful servant" (Matthew 25:23). This requires us to be able to do two things concerning salvation: (1) live in obedience and holiness, making right moral choices., and (2) glory in Jesus Christ and His grace, saying with conviction that God *has* saved us, God is *saving* us, and God one day *will* save us.

Weslyan Methodist doctrine of heaven and hell

The eighteenth century revival led by John and Charles Wesley brought hundreds of thousands of sinners to believe in Christ and receive salvation by faith. John Wesley sometimes said he was passing through this life "as an arrow through the air." This life was a precursor to the next, and the most significant question for a person was whether this life's trajectory ended in heaven or hell. Wesley believed in a traditional view of heaven and hell. Because God was just, and humans were sinners, unless they availed themselves of the forgiveness made possible by Jesus Christ, they would face an angry God when they died. He encouraged his listeners to "flee the wrath to come." Hell, according to Wesley, was a real place of real torment that lasted through eternity. Heaven, in contrast, was a place of pleasure, not sensual, but the blessedness of being in the presence of God. What salvation means is to be free of sin and thus able to live in the presence of God. This presence is available to believers in this life but is available fully and directly in the life to come.

Methodists have historically differed from Presbyterians in believing that the believer can approach sinless perfection, and in believing that if they do not make progress toward perfection, they can lose their salvation. While in the past these differences about your ability to accept salvation, and to live a sinless life or lose salvation, have distinguished Methodists from other Protestants, in more recent years the deeper significant split has been between the more conservative and more liberal wings of each Protestant denomination. Conservative Methodists and conservative Presbyterians resemble each other more than conservative and liberal Methodists do, and the same is true for the liberal wings.

The conservative wing of the Methodist Church maintains its belief in an afterlife spent in a literal place, either heaven or hell. More liberal Methodists tend to downplay hell, often because the image of God torturing people for eternity, even if they are sinners, is not easy to square with their idea of a loving God. Nor is it easy for them to square the idea of a just God with one who casts people into hell because, as the result of fortune for which they are not responsible, they have not lived in a place where the Gospel of Jesus was preached

Calvinism and hell

The following is extracted from John Calvin's brief teaching on Hell in *Institutes of the Christian Religion* (1559), Book 3, Chapter 25, Section 12.

As language cannot describe the severity of the divine vengeance on the reprobate, their pains and torments are figured to us by corporeal things, such as darkness, wailing and gnashing of teeth, inextinguishable fire, the ever-gnawing worm (Matthew 8:12; 22:13; Mark 9:43; Isaiah 66:24). It is certain that by such modes of expression the Holy Spirit designed to impress all our senses with dread, as when it is said, "Tophet is ordained of old; yea, for the king it is prepared: he has made it deep and large; the pile thereof is fire and much wood; the breath of the Lord, like a stream of brimstone, does kindle it" (Isaiah 30:33). As we thus require to be assisted to conceive the miserable doom of the reprobate, so the consideration on which we ought chiefly to dwell is the fearful consequence of being estranged from all fellowship with God, and not only so, but of feeling that His majesty is adverse to us, while we cannot possibly escape from it. For, first, His indignation is like a raging fire, by whose touch all things are devoured and annihilated. Next, all the creatures are the instruments of His judgment, so that those to whom the Lord will thus publicly manifest His anger will feel that Heaven, and Earth, and sea, all beings, animate and inanimate, are, as it were, inflamed with dire indignation against them, and armed for their destruction. Wherefore, the Apostle made no trivial declaration, when he said that unbelievers shall be "punished with everlasting destruction from the presence of the Lord, and from the glory of His power" (2 Thessalonians 1:9). And whenever the prophets strike terror by means of corporeal figures, although in respect of our dull understanding there is no extravagance in their language, yet they give preludes of the future judgment in the sun and the moon, and the whole fabric of the world. Hence unhappy consciences find no rest but are vexed and driven about by a dire whirlwind, feeling as if torn by an angry God, pierced through with deadly darts, terrified by His thunderbolts and crushed by the weight of His hand; so that it were easier to plunge into abysses and whirlpools than endure these terrors for a moment. How fearful, then, must it be to be thus beset throughout eternity! On this subject there is a memorable passage in the ninetieth Psalm: Although God by a mere look scatters all mortals, and brings them to nought, yet as His worshippers are more timid in this world, He urges them the more, that He may stimulate them, while burdened with the cross to press onward until He himself shall be all in all.

This seems to propose a doctrine of annihilation where the punishment is dust and ashes for the sinner. This would preclude eternal torment and a conscious awareness of eternal punishment. This view is not acceptable to most evangelicals as it is not Biblical. The Bible, and solid Biblical proof texts, is what they rely on for the doctrine of eternal punishment.

Thomas Aquinas – Summa Theologica

"The magnitude of the punishment matches the magnitude of the sin. Now a sin that is against God is infinite; the higher the person against whom it is committed, the graver the sin – it is more criminal to strike a head of state than a private citizen – and God is of infinite greatness. Therefore, an infinite punishment is deserved for a sin committed against Him."

Relationships not rationality

Christianity inherited the Jewish cosmology, but almost from the beginning of the religion, as early as Paul's letters; the adherents associated Christ with the creative work of the Father. He is *"the one Lord through whom all things exist and by whom we are"* (1 Corinthians 8:6). *He is the Wisdom of God* (1 Corinthians 1:24), *"the image of the invisible God and the first-born of all creatures; in whom all things were made and now exist"* (Colossians 1:15).

Furthermore, creation now has its end and purpose in him, Christ. Therefore, and not surprisingly so, Evangelical Christian interest in cosmology and creation has changed from being concerned with matter or technique to one of relationship, that is, a dependency on the creator not only for his creation but also for its subsistence. The General Thanksgiving in the Book of Common Prayer encourages Christians to give thanks for our creation, preservation, and all blessings of this life:-

Thanksgiving Prayer (iv)

Accept, O Lord,
our thanks and praise for all that you have done for us.
We thank you for the splendour of the whole creation,
for the beauty of this world, for the wonder of life, and for the
    mystery of love.
We thank you for the blessing of family and friends,
and for the loving care which surrounds us on every side.
We thank you for setting us at tasks which demand our
    best efforts,
and for leading us to accomplishments which satisfy and
    delight us.
We thank you also for those disappointments and failures
that lead us to acknowledge our dependence on you alone.
Above all, we thank you for your Son Jesus Christ;

for the truth of his Word and the example of his life; for his
steadfast obedience,
by which he overcame temptation; for his dying, through
which he overcame death;
and for his rising to life again, in which we are raised to the
life of your kingdom.
Grant us the gift of your Spirit, that we may know him and
make him known;
and through him, at all times and in all places, may give
thanks to you in all things.
Amen.

Creation and preservation are the same thing. The creativity of
God is continuous: if God as the creator withdrew his creative
presence from an entity, it would cease to exist. Therefore,
according to this theological thinking God is not just the cause
of all things, past, present, and future, but he is the essence of
their being. Heaven, therefore would be where God is

Conclusion

"For millennia the basic Christian cosmological concept has
remained a three-status universe: heaven above, earth in the
middle, and hell below. Even though alternative cosmologies
have been suggested to reflect changes produced from scientific
knowledge, the main theological concept remains. However,
such suggestions have caused a distinction to be made between
God, the first cause above, who produces and sustains creation
in which both natural and free causes, secondary causes,
operate, and those effective and efficient causes which are real
and not normal." **(v)**

Biblical Cosmology

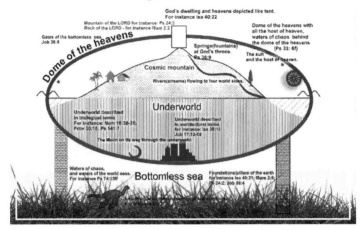

Bibliography
i.   Jeffrey Kranz – www.overviewbible.com 9th August 2018

ii.   Biblical cosmology – Wikipedia, the free encyclopedia
www//en.wikipedia.org/wiki/Biblical cosmology

iii. (Barth – Dogmatics p64)

iv. ~ from the *Book of Common Prayer/Book of Divine Worship*. Posted on **ChurchYear.net** http://www. churchyear.net/thanks.html

v.   (Bowker, John, The Oxford Dictionary of World Religions, New York, Oxford University Press, 1997, p. 239)

CHAPTER SIX

Eschatology of heaven and hell

*Eschatology – NOUN: the part of theology
concerned with death, judgement, and the final
destiny of the soul and of humankind. "Christian
hope is concerned with eschatology, or the
science of last things"*

*"God never takes away something from your life
without replacing it with something better."*
– Billy Graham **(i)**

*"We may speak about a place where there are no
tears, no death, no fear, no night; but those are
just the benefits of heaven. The beauty of heaven
is seeing God"* – Max Lucado **(ii)**

Introduction

At theological college one of the student jokes about the study
of eschatology was that we didn't have the time for it! Ironically
the essence of eschatology is time, then, now and yet to come.
So much of the prophetic scriptures is centred upon this theme.
Prophets see the image in the 'now' as pointing to the completed
picture in a time which is yet to come. Even Jesus speaks of

this using this language in his conversation with the Samaritan woman in John 4: 21-23. *Woman," Jesus replied, "believe me, a time is coming when you will worship the Father neither on this mountain nor in Jerusalem. You Samaritans worship what you do not know; we worship what we do know, for salvation is from the Jews. Yet a time is coming and has now come when the true worshipers will worship the Father in the Spirit and in truth, for they are the kind of worshipers the Father seeks.* Jesus, in this conversation talks of a time yet to come when all people will no longer worship the Father in an earthly place, even though the Jews know whom they worship, but in a spiritual relationship in the kingdom of heaven (verse 23 suggests both Jew and gentile if they are true worshipers).

St Paul too, uses this eschatological language in his letter to the Roman church. He talks in Chapter eight of 'present sufferings, future glory'. This is the context for all that he is about to teach the church. In Romans 8:18-25 we read *"I consider that our present sufferings are not worth comparing with the glory that will be revealed in us. For the creation waits in eager expectation for the children of God to be revealed. For the creation was subjected to frustration, not by its own choice, but by the will of the one who subjected it, in hope that the creation itself will be liberated from its bondage to decay and brought into the freedom and glory of the children of God. We know that the whole creation has been groaning as in the pains of childbirth right up to the present time. Not only so, but we ourselves, who have the first fruits of the Spirit, groan inwardly as we wait eagerly for our adoption to sonship, the redemption of our bodies. For in this hope we were saved. But hope that is seen is no hope at all. Who hopes for what they already have? But if we hope for what we do not yet have, we wait for it patiently".*

John Wesley is recorded to have cried out on his death bed "the best is yet to be" and then lifting a thin arm up to heaven he repeated what he had just said before dying attended by his friends. **(iii)** John Wesley believed that he was going to heaven and would inherit eternal life. In a similar way a Christian man who lived in Normanton, a mining community near Wakefield in Yorkshire, caused a stir by riding his bike through the town singing, "I am coming Lord, coming Lord to thee". Not long afterwards he passed away to join his Lord in heaven. Both men, one a learned clergyman and the other a former miner, knew by faith, where they were going after death, and who they would be with. They both lived by faith ready for 'not yet'!

Old Testament Eschatology

The Old Testament prophets particularly bring eschatological hope first for Israel and then for all people. The prophet Jeremiah writes:

"In those days people will no longer say, 'The parents have eaten sour grapes, and the children's teeth are set on edge'." *Instead, everyone will die for their own sin; whoever eats sour grapes – their own teeth will be set on edge. 'The days are coming,' declares the Lord, 'when I will make a new covenant with the people of Israel and with the people of Judah. It will not be like the covenant I made with their ancestors when I took them by the hand to lead them out of Egypt, because they broke my covenant, though I was a husband to them,' declares the Lord. 'This is the covenant that I will make with the people of Israel after that time,' declares the LORD. 'I will put my law in their minds and write it on their hearts. I will be their God, and they will be my people. No longer will they teach their neighbour, or say to one another, "Know the LORD," because they will all know me, from the least of them to the greatest,' declares the LORD. 'For I will forgive their wickedness and will remember their sins no more.'* (Jeremiah 31:29-34 cf. Ezekiel 18; 36:25-27). Jeremiah is speaking about the new and personal covenant to be made through the blood of Jesus shed on the cross. It is important therefore that, in our eschatology, we remember this individual emphasis and do not just

emphasise Israel as a nation. We must be careful to speak about an Israel in which individuals know the Lord personally and have the law written on their hearts and minds. It must be Israel which has turned to Christ. This cannot be fulfilled until the time (eschaton) when "all Israel will be saved" as Paul writes in Rom 11:26.

There are also a series of supernatural promises contained in the Old Testament that are all about the future (eschaton). These in brief are,

(i)   Israel will return from exile around the world (Isa 51:11; Jeremiah 30:10-20; Ezekiel 36:22-28, 33; 37; Zephaniah 3:9-20)

(ii) There will be an attack on Israel. Ezekiel predicts the invasion of Israel by Gog, an army probably led by Russia. (Ezekiel 38/39). The prophet Zechariah predicts that all the nations will attack Jerusalem (Zechariah 12:1-3; 14:1-2) and that two thirds of the people will be struck down (Zechariah 13:8-9).

(iii) The Church of God, the One New Man of Ephesians 2, will be caught up with Jesus in the air to receive their rewards and enjoy the Banquet of the Lamb (1 Thessalonians 4; John 14:1-6: Revelation 19)

(iv) There will be seven years of Tribulation. Jeremiah calls it "a time of trouble for Jacob" (Jeremiah 30:7).

(v)   Israel will turn to Jesus as their Messiah and Lord (Zechariah 12:10-13:1)

(vi) The anti-Christ will arise and be defeated in Israel at the Battle of Armageddon (Revelation 19:20) ready for the Final Judgement (Daniel 11:36). [For more detail see the Timeline in Appendix A].

(vii) The Lord Jesus will return to earth on the Mount of Olives at His second coming. (Daniel 7:13-14)

(viii) The Lord will bring judgement on the unrepentant sinners and blessings for the redeemed (Isaiah 11:4 cf. 24:1-12, 17-23; 26:20f; 27:1; 34:1-4; 63:1-6; Obadiah15-16; Zechariah 14:3, 12-15)

(ix) The Lord will reign on this present earth for 1000 years

(x) There will be a day of Judgement for all the dead unbelievers when their works and lives are checked against the Lamb's Book of Life (Revelation 20:11-15)

(xi) There will then be, at last, a New Heaven and New Earth (Revelation 21:1-4)

(xii) We will be with Jesus in His eternal kingdom of heaven (which will be the New Jerusalem) and will reign with Him for ever. (Revelation 21:1-6)

This is by no means an exhaustive list but illustrates the prophetic nature of God's words to Israel in the Old Testament through the prophets. How amazing that Israel has, in a one-day miracle, returned to the land, Halleluiah! When Israel became a nation state on 14th May 1948, it really was a case of the impossible becoming reality. It was also the cornerstone prophetic event of human history and had been foretold over and over by the Old Testament prophets. The Jews are the only ancient people group to survive to modern times. Yet paradoxically, they are the most persecuted people in history. Despite the murderous threats of their enemies, Israel continues to thrive. The story of the birth of the modern state of Israel is a story like no other; a real-life miracle that will encourage you and can build your faith. A Nation was born in a day as prophesied by the Old Testament prophet Isaiah. Some 2,750 years later, on 14th May 1948, his prophecy came true, when the present-day nation State of Israel was born. **(iv)** The eminent British historian Paul Johnson wrote of the Jewish State: "In the last half-century, over 100 completely new independent states have come into existence. Israel is the only one whose creation can fairly be called a miracle." Israel is a miracle because the Jewish state was established against all odds. **(v)**

New Testament Eschatology

Eschatology comes from the Greek ἔσχατος = eskhatos, meaning "last, final" or escaton pantwn (Mark 12:22 & 1 Corinthians 15:8) meaning 'last of all', which makes sense as this branch of theology is the study of the 'End Times' **(v)** particularly life or death. More specifically, eschatology involves four elements or "last" things: death, judgment, heaven and hell. Evangelical theology (which I believe to be correct) includes the Rapture, The Great Tribulation, the Millennium, end of the world, the last judgment, a new heaven and a new earth as detailed in Chapter Six (the World to Come), and the ultimate consummation of all of God's purpose. Wow! Maranatha! Come Lord Jesus (Revelation 22:20)

The eschatological reality of heaven is eternal life in heaven, worshipping God and the Lamb, in the light of His holy presence. This is where the redeemed are heading, whereas the unsaved dead and unrepentant sinner will find his or her eschatological reality is the second death in the Lake of Fire, where torment and anguish surround them for ever. What was partly understood by the Jews and explained by their prophets was a future reality of either heaven or hell. One day soon that reality will be known. For the Christian this has been clearly expressed in the New Testament and has become a promise sealed in the blood of Jesus. We are commanded by Scripture to keep the words of prophecy in Scripture and to worship God (Revelation 22:7,9). The warnings are made clear. In Revelation 22:10-11 we read *"Then he told me, "Do not seal up the words of the prophecy of this scroll, because the time is near. Let the one who does wrong continue to do wrong; let the vile person continue to be vile; let the one who does right continue to do right; and let the holy person continue to be holy."* And a few verses later in Revelation 22:14-15 Jesus says [4]*"Blessed are those who wash their robes, that they may have the right to the tree of life and may go through the gates into the city. Outside are the dogs, those who practice magic arts, the sexually immoral, the murderers, the idolaters and everyone who loves and practices falsehood".* This is eternal separation – the final reality for those who turned down God's gracious offer of salvation. After death there is no second chance (Hebrews 9:27)

We shall look at a timeline of these events in the next chapter but first let us consider what heaven itself holds for us. Our information comes largely from the Revelation to the Apostle John. Consider this picture taken from Revelation 4:1-11; 5:12-14 & 7:9-17. Heaven is very full! It is full of worship and praise and it is awe of Jesus, the Lamb of God and the Lion of Judah.

In a fulfilment of Micaiah's prophecy to the King of Israel (1 Kings 22:19) the host of heaven is described in detail in the book of Revelation. There are twenty-four elders (representing the Old Testament and New Testament Saints), seven spirits of God, four living creatures, mighty angels and ten thousand times ten thousand angels and unnumbered saints, not forgetting the focus of their worship Jesus Lamb of God and Lion of Judah! We are told that it is a great multitude that no-one can count – it sure is! How ironic that the King of Israel said to King Jehoshaphat of Micaiah, "he never prophecies anything good about me, only bad." If only the King of Israel had believed this good and true prophetic word (1 Kings 22:8,18)

The Revelation of heaven to the Apostle John, also confirmed heaven as a living and alive place, full of holy beings worshipping and praising God. John is invited to go up to heaven (Revelation 4:1) *"Come up here, and I will show you what must take place after this".* Heaven is both physical and spiritual (Revelation 4:2) and it is a place of silence and awe (Revelation 8:1). The Revelation to John also reveals that heaven is a place of:

(i) Flashes of lightening and peals of thunder (Revelation 4:5)

(ii) Supernatural signs like the four living creatures and the exalted army of angelic beings (Revelation 4:6-8)

(iii) Glory (cf Psalm 19:1)

(iv) Departure for Satan who was cast down to earth for his rebellion against God (Revelation 12:9) and who will, after being summoned by God, be hurled down in eternal exclusion with his angels to await the imprisonment in the abyss and their eternal torment in the Lake of Fire (see also Isaiah 14:12 & Luke 10:18)

(v) God's dwelling (Deuteronomy 26:15 & 1 Kings 8:30)

We can see that this revelation of heaven is clearly not of 'here and now'. It is of a 'not yet' and thus of another 'eschatos' or time. This kingdom is the kingdom of heaven; a kingdom rejected by the Jews at Jesus' first coming, but which will be restored to the believing Jews at the second advent. Matthew's gospel is very much about the Saviour King and His kingdom and so we find the gospel account exclusively focussing on the 'kingdom of heaven' (e.g. Matthew 3:2; 4:17; 5:3; 5:10; 5:19; 11:11 etc over 24 times). The eschatological nature of the kingdom is shown by Jesus words in Matthew 4:17 calling people to repent and believe in him because *"for the kingdom of heaven is near"*. This kingdom is the coming kingdom to be inaugurated at Jesus second advent and is not the military victory over the Romans that many Jews expected. This promise of a future kingdom is made by Jesus for people of all ages. In Matthew 19:14 he says, *"The kingdom of heaven belongs to such as these"* (i.e. children). In the kingdom of heaven Jesus will sit at the right hand of God (Mark 16:19). This kingdom of heaven is also the place where Jesus came from to earth (John 6:38) and where he will come again from at His second coming.

In St Paul's second letter to the Corinthians he talks about his experience after having been stoned to death at Lystra (Acts 14:19-20). His testimony is, that after death he was taken up to the third heaven (2 Corinthians 12:1-10). In other words, he was taken up to the place of God's abode, the highest heaven (Psalm 115:16), or paradise (see Luke 16:19-31) and it was his testimony that in heaven he heard inexpressible things that he could not talk about in this life.

In the letter to the Hebrews we find that our heavenly calling (Hebrews 3:1) is the longing of the saints (Hebrews 11:15) and that this longing for heaven is emphasised throughout the letter. Our citizenship says 'St Paul' is in heaven (Philippians 3:20) "But our citizenship is in heaven. And we eagerly await a Saviour from there, the Lord Jesus Christ."

The Millennial kingdom on earth is the thousand-year reign of Christ with His saints, whereas the Kingdom of heaven is eternal, that is, part present and future.

Conclusion

Heaven and hell are eschatological realities as both places exist and are key to the plan of God and the hope of mankind for peace, love, life in all its fullness and the presence of, on the one hand God and the other hand nothing. Scripture bears witness to this and God's grace makes the one a reality and His divine judgement makes the other an eternal torment. From one point of view this aspect of God's character is shown in that he does not want anyone to perish (2 Peter 3:9) and on the other hand He has already provided the means of being saved (John 3:16-17). No wonder then that as the Israelites wandered in the wilderness, Moses was commanded to tell them that a choice had to be made about their eternal destination. In

Deuteronomy 30:19 God told Moses to tell the Israelites *"This day I call the heavens and the earth as witnesses against you that I have set before you life and death, blessings and curses. Now choose life, so that you and your children may live"*. Let us thank God for his offer of eternal life and ask His help that we too can make the right choice, for, in the words of St Paul, we can then confidently hope for the kingdom of heaven. This hope *"does not disappoint us, because God has poured out His love into our hearts by the Holy Spirit whom He has given us"* (Romans 5:5)

Here is a very powerful review of David Jeremiah's book "Answers to your questions about heaven" **(vi).** The reviewer said "I was intrigued by the questions shared in the Answers to Your Questions about Heaven, but I would not need to read it again. This book made me go back to Hebrews 11:1 – "Now faith is confidence in what we hope for and assurance about what we do not see." Faith builds hope and trust and removes worry. So, I don't need to worry about heaven. God has kept his promises for ages past, I know he will keep his promise of heaven to me." To this we can say **Amen and thank you Lord.**

On a different note regarding 'heaven' and on this I will end this chapter, I liked Bill Johnson's book "When Heaven invades earth". The sub title is 'A Practical Guide to a Life of Miracles'. This gives the reader a solid clue as to the thrust of the book. The number of endorsements written by Church pastors and leaders is very impressive as is the range of comments and theology. Whilst the book doesn't present a theological argument about heaven or hell, it nevertheless makes a very serious point about the kingdom of heaven in the here and now. Bill Johnson's thesis is that the miracles and ministry of the Holy Spirit represents the reality of God's kingdom, and that God's kingdom is easily and quickly extended by it. Eschatologically speaking the kingdom has come in Jesus and is here being demonstrated among us. It is a challenging thought. In the words of Cal Pierce, Director, Healing Rooms

Ministries "The book releases revelation into the army of God that moves it into the kingdom work. Bill Johnson shows us that the kingdom of God isn't just a future kingdom, but a kingdom work that is available here and now". May God graciously let us experience His kingdom too in this way that faith may rise in His church and the kingdom be revealed. **Amen.**

End Notes:

i. **The Heaven Answer Book:** Billy Graham – Billy Graham Evangelistic Association

ii. **Experiencing the Heart of Jesus: Knowing His Heart, Feeling His love**: Max Lucado – Thomas Nelson

iii. **The Journal of John Wesley:** ed Percy Livingstone Park – Chicago Moody Press

iv. **The Miracle that is Israel**: Phil Davies – Resources for Church

v. https://www.frontpagemag.com/fpm/95512/miracle-israel-joseph-puder

vi. **Answers to your questions about heaven**: David Jeremiah – Tyndale House Publishers inc 2015

CHAPTER SEVEN

God's timeline for the coming heaven and hell

If patience is worth anything, it must endure to the **end of time**. *And a living faith will last in the midst of the blackest storm.* – Mohandas Gandhi

"The good die first, And they whose hearts are dry as summer dust Burn to the socket."
William Wordsworth (1770-1850) from his poem
"The Excursion":

The position that this book takes regarding God's timeline for heaven and hell is that of a Pre-Tribulation Rapture in which view the Second coming of Christ follows immediately at the end of the seven-year Tribulation. The Second coming of Christ ushers in the Millennium period of Christ's rule and reign from Jerusalem. A deep theological question then arises, namely, is the Millennium period 'heaven on earth'? or is it one thousand years of peace and justice with Jesus ruling and reigning over all the earth helped by the Saints, who have been appointed to rule and reign with Him and come back with Him for that purpose?

There are some important definitions to be aware of when considering the End Times. Some of these, like Rapture, 144,000, Millennium, and tribulation are dealt with in Gods Glorious Promise (i) and some, like eschatology, in this book. Others require stating here in order to help with understanding this chapter as follows:

Armageddon: (taken from the Hebrew *Har-Megiddon*, Mount Megiddo). The city of Megiddo was situated between the Plain of Jezreel and the western coast of Israel. Deborah, Gideon, Saul, Ahaziah, and Josiah fought decisive battles near Megiddo. So, the valley of Megiddo became the symbol of a point of decisive conflict. Based upon the reference to Armageddon in Revelation 16:16, some theologians believe that a literal battle will occur near Megiddo whilst others understand this reference to be a symbol of the ultimate conflict between good and evil.

Anti-Christ: (taken from the Greek, antichristos, in place of Christ) means anyone who denies the Apostles teaching about Jesus Christ (1 John2:18-22; 2 John 1:7). Specifically, the anti-Christ is a satanic counterfeit of Jesus Christ, described as 'lawless' (2 Thessalonians 2:3-8) and as a 'beast' (Revelation 13:1-18; 17:3-17). The anti-Christ may be a specific person who rises to power during the Tribulation or it may be a symbol of the false teachers and leaders who will arise when the End Times draw near.

Mark of the beast: the indication of person's allegiance to anti-Christ (Revelation 13:16-17). Some premillennialists believe that the mark of the beast will be an actual mark required by the anti-Christ. Others argue that it is a reference to a person's deeds (hand) and beliefs (forehead) as suggested by Exodus 13:9,16.

When we are considering the differing views of the Millennium, we should bear in mind that these views are

124

influenced by what theologian's call "Schools of Interpretation". There are four widely agreed schools and these are: preterist; historicist; futurist and idealist.

Preterist" means past in fulfilment (particularly during the rise and fall of the Roman Empire), and "Futurist" means future in fulfilment. Preterist basically means the opposite of Futurist and this interpretation was used in the first century AD to prepare Christians for what was to come on the second and third centuries. Futurists believe most end-time prophecies (especially the big three events – the Second Coming, Resurrection, and Judgment) are yet to be fulfilled until the second half of the Great Tribulation. The focus of futurists is therefore on a three-and-a-half-year period in the second half of the Tribulation, and just before the Second coming. Preterists believe that most or all of Bible Prophecy (especially the big three events) has already been fulfilled in Christ and the on-going expansion of His Eternal Kingdom. Many Futurists do not really believe that Christ has been successful in fully establishing His Kingdom.

The Preterist interpretation of Bible prophecy is capturing significant media attention, and according to one critic, is "spreading like wildfire" in the social media. It is compatible with the essential beliefs of all Christians and is already represented in nearly all Protestant denominations and the Roman Catholic Church. It has been mentioned several times in publications such as Christianity Today, Christian News, Great Christian Books catalogue, World Magazine, and several others.

Historicism is an approach to eschatology and prophecy in general. In historicism, biblical prophecies are interpreted as representative of literal historical events. Historicism looks at the whole of Bible prophecy as a sweeping overview of church history, from Pentecost to the end times. This approach involves interpreting symbols or figures in the Bible as metaphors for actual events, nations, or persons of history. Historicism was especially popular during the Reformation, when it was used to suggest that the Catholic Church was part of the end-times apostasy, with the pope as the Antichrist.

Idealism (also called the spiritual approach, the allegorical approach, the nonliteral approach, and many other names) in Christian eschatology is an interpretation of the Book of Revelation that sees all of the imagery of the book as non-literal symbols. In other words, it treats Revelation as myth, that is, spiritually true but not historically true. For a fuller discussion on all four interpretations see "When Jesus Returns" **(ii)**

Traditionally there have been four views of the Millennium, which is, of course the reign of Christ on earth as described in Revelation 20:4-6. **(iii)**

The four views present quite different ideas about heaven and the Millennium. The first view is called **Historic Premillennialism**. It can be represented by the following diagram.

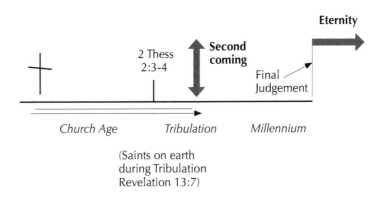

(Saints on earth
during Tribulation
Revelation 13:7)

Historic Premillennialism seems to have been the earliest view of the End Times among post-apostolic Christians including Irenaeus (130-200AD); Justin Martyr (100-165AD) and Papias (60-130AD). In more recent times this view has been championed by theologians like George Beasley-Murray.

It is very hard to understand what the Millennium kingdom of Christ would be like in this view. Without a clear break between the reign of the anti-Christ and of Jesus, it is hard to see how the millennium reign of Jesus could be like heaven. In addition, the salvation of the Jews and the 'One New Man' of Jew and Gentile together and the defeat of Israel's enemies must be part of any millennium reign for this period to be like heaven.

The second view would be that of **Dispensational Premillennialism** which emerged in 1800's among the Plymouth Brethren and is supported by Church leaders like J Nelson Derby, Hal Lindsay and Tim Lahaye. This view is based upon scripture like Genesis 15:18, *"On that day the LORD made a covenant with Abram and said, 'To your descendants I give this land, from the Wadi of Egypt to the great river, the Euphrates'"* and other Covenant promises of God regarding the promised Land, made to Abraham, Isaac and Jacob. In addition, this view takes passages like Revelation 4:1-2 to refer to the Rapture (1 Thessalonians 4:16-17) through which Jesus takes His church from the earth before the Tribulation begins. Further evidence of this is found in 1 Thessalonians 5:9 and Revelation 3:10. This view also anticipates that during the Tribulation many Jews will turn to Christ and be saved and that, because the church is not mentioned in the Book of Revelation after Chapter 4, that references to Israel mean the nation of Israel. This view can be represented by the following diagram.

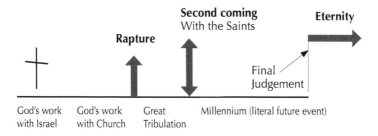

Second coming
With the Saints

Eternity

Rapture

Final
Judgement

God's work   God's work   Great   Millennium (literal future event)
with Israel   with Church   Tribulation

Some Christians who believe in a Dispensational Premillennialism believe that the Rapture does not occur at the beginning of the Great tribulation but in the middle of it. Not surprisingly they are known as mid-tribulationists. Although the reign of Jesus in the Millennium will be more like heaven there will still be the problem of many unsaved and saints being alive together and thus preventing the eternal kingdom as defined in the previous chapter.

The third view is called **Amillennialism** and believes that from the Resurrection and after the Ascension, Christ reigns in Christians until His second coming (Revelation 19:11-21).

This view became popular in the fifth century and is said to have been the view of St Augustine of Hippo. In more recent years great Protestant reformers have taken this view. These include Martin Luther and John Calvin and latterly John Packer.

Those who hold this view also believe that during the same time frame the world sees an increase in evil and that the Great tribulation represents the calamities and persecutions experienced by Christians trying to live their lives in obedience to Christ. Thus this view, like the first view, believes that the saints will be on earth during the Tribulation period (Revelation 13:7). How that view works timewise when the Tribulation is a period of seven years and the Millennium is 1000 years is not really explained. This view also takes a 'spiritualised' view of the first resurrection "*I saw thrones on which were seated those who had been given authority to judge. And I saw the souls of those who had been beheaded because of their testimony about Jesus and because of the word of God. They had not worshiped the beast or its image and had not received its mark on their foreheads or their hands. They came to life and reigned with Christ a thousand years*". (Revelation 20:4). Amillennialists believe that the Second coming of Christ and the resurrection of the saved and unsaved will occur at the same time (Daniel 12:2-3). They also believe that the first resurrection (Revelation 20:4) could refer to the spiritual resurrection and therefore be the moment of new birth. In John 3:1-8 we read *"Now there was a Pharisee, a man named Nicodemus who was a member of the Jewish ruling council. He came to Jesus at night and said, "Rabbi, we know that you are a teacher who has come from God. For no one could perform the signs you are doing if God were not with him." Jesus replied, "Very truly I tell you, no one can see the kingdom of God unless they are born again." "How can someone be born when they are old?" Nicodemus asked. "Surely they cannot enter a second time into their mother's womb to be born!" Jesus answered, "Very truly I tell you, no one can enter the kingdom of God unless they are born of water and the Spirit. Flesh gives birth to flesh, but the Spirit gives birth to spirit. You should not be surprised at my saying, 'You must be born again.' The wind blows wherever it pleases. You hear its sound, but you cannot tell where it comes from or where it is going. So it is with everyone born of the Spirit."* Alternatively, they argue that it could mean those who trust Christ, *"I am talking to you Gentiles. Inasmuch as I am the apostle to the Gentiles, I take pride in my ministry in the hope that I may somehow arouse my own people to envy and save some of them. For if their rejection brought reconciliation to the world, what will their acceptance be but life from the dead?"* (Romans 11:13-15)

This view can be represented by the following diagram:

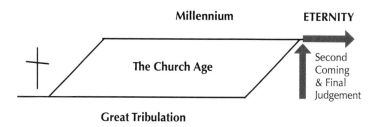

The Final view is called **Postmillennialism.** This view is shared by 19th century theologians and preachers like Charles Spurgeon and theologians like R C Sproul. Simply put this view believes that the Second coming coincides with the end of the Millennium and the Final Judgement. In this view the Church Age runs into the Tribulation and then the Millennium but, unlike the first two views, believes that society gradually improves during the period following Pentecost to the Second Coming. This is at odds with Jesus own description of the End Times before he returns in which he describes the increase in wickedness and evil, the falling away from faith and the natural signs (see God's Glorious Promise **(iv)**) and Where are we Heading, Heaven Only Knows **(v)**). In this view it is also believed that the Second Coming and the resurrection of all people, saved and unsaved, will occur at the same time. *"Multitudes who sleep in the dust of the earth will awake: some to everlasting life, others to shame and everlasting contempt. Those who are wise will shine like the brightness of the heavens, and those who lead many to righteousness, like the stars for ever and ever"* (Daniel 12:2-3) and *"Do not be amazed at this, for a time is coming when all who are in their graves will hear His voice and come out-those who have done what is good will rise to live, and those who have done what is evil will rise to be condemned* (John 5:28-29).

Proponents of this view also do not believe that Jesus will be on the earth during the Millennium but that He will rule through the Church by His Spirit and that the resurrection depicted in Revelation 20:4 represents the spiritual regeneration of people who trust Jesus. They also believe that the Second Coming is the final conflict between good and evil, the defeat of Satan and the physical resurrection of all people (Romans 11:13-15 and Ephesians 2:1-4). In their view the Final Judgement will occur at the Second Coming immediately after the Millennium (Revelation 20:7-15). The following diagram shows this position.

God's timeline for the coming heaven and hell

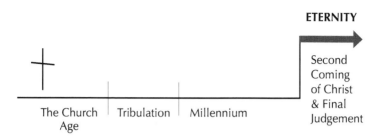

ETERNITY

The Church Age | Tribulation | Millennium | Second Coming of Christ & Final Judgement

Another End Times Calendar, and one which I support, is like the Dispensational Millennium view above but where three decisive battles occur at or just after the Rapture, The Second Coming and just before the Great White throne Judgement. This view is represented by the diagram shown in Appendix A. (from God's Glorious Promise – see below)

End Notes:

i. **God's Glorious Promise**: Andrew Baguley and Roger French – New Wine

ii. **When Jesus Returns:** David Pawson – Hodder & Stoughton

iii. Taken from "Four Views of the Millennium" 2000 Rose Publishing USA

iv. **God's Glorious Promise**: Andrew Baguley and Roger French – New Wine

v. **Where are We heading? Heaven only Knows!**: Andrew Baguley – Lighthouse Publications

CHAPTER EIGHT

A testimony of visiting heaven

*Blessed assurance, Jesus is mine! O what a
foretaste of glory divine! Heir of salvation,
purchase of God, born of his Spirit, washed in
his blood. Refrain: This is my story, this is my
song, praising my Saviour all the day long; this is
my story, this is my song, praising my Saviour all
the day long. Perfect submission, perfect delight,
visions of rapture now burst on my sight; angels
descending bring from above echoes of mercy,
whispers of love. (Refrain)* – Fanny J Crosby
(1820 – 1915)

*If you come back from the dead, you don't
have the same value system, I think.*
– Sigourney Weaver b1949

Daniel Ecechuckwa: Testimony is of a Nigerian pastor who died
and rose again. (i)

Pastor Daniel Ekeckukwu (Dan Eke) is the Senior Pastor at
Voice of Resurrection Ministries, East London, Eastern Cape,
South Africa. In 2001, the Nigerian-born Pastor died and was
raised from the dead in Onitsha, Anambra, Eastern Nigeria.

For the days he was dead on earth, his spirit had encounters in heaven and hell. But as his amazing story of his life shows, before he was called to serve God, he lived a life of hell on earth. Daniel Ekechukwu died in a car accident and was taken to heaven and hell by two large angels. This testimony is important because it highlights the importance of forgiveness. Had God not given him mercy, Daniel would have had to stay in hell because he did not forgive his wife prior to death.

On Thursday, November 29th, 2001, Pastor Daniel Ekechukwu and his wife, Nneka, had a misunderstanding that degenerated into an argument that ended in her slapping him. He was very offended by this incident, to the point of not even acknowledging her attempt to reconcile the next morning. Pastor Daniel admitted that throughout the day of November 30th, he angrily thought about how he would put his wife in her place when he returned home. He would not, however, make it home that Friday.

As he was driving home that evening, the brakes on his 20-year old Mercedes 230E failed as he was heading down a steep hill, and his car crashed into a concrete pillar that was built to prevent cars from going over a steep embankment. He was not wearing a seat belt, and his chest hit very forcibly against the steering wheel and its knob, apparently doing damage to his internal organs, as he was soon vomiting up blood and having difficulty breathing. Daniel was not able to remove himself from his car, but frantic on-lookers pulled him out. One bystander volunteered her car while another bystander offered to drive him to St. Charles Borromeo Hospital, not far away on the outskirts of Onitsha.

Within minutes of their arrival at the hospital, a doctor began administering emergency treatment, but Daniel knew his body was not responding to it. He began praying the prayer of a man who knows he is going to die, asking God to forgive him of all his sins so that he would be ready to stand before the Lord. He also sent for his wife, Nneka, with whom he had refused to speak when he left his home earlier that day. She fainted upon hearing the news of her husband's accident and condition, but when revived was taken by a Christian neighbour to the hospital. Daniel's friend, Ede Samuel was with her and witnessed everything that transpired over the next three days.

Upon seeing Daniel in critical condition when she arrived at St. Charles Borromeo hospital, Daniel's wife burst into tears, begging her husband not to die and leave her. The doctor admitted that there was nothing he could do to save Daniel's life, and so Daniel requested that he be transferred by ambulance to Umezuruike Hospital at Owerri, where his personal doctor practiced. The Umezuruike hospital was 80 km away. Daniel's wife arranged for the ambulance against the advice of doctors at St. Charles hospital. It was on the way to Umezuruike Hospital that Daniel died.

Daniel was lying in the back of the ambulance while his wife was in the front passenger seat. He began to feel that he was not going to survive, and so he called for his wife to come to him. He began to say goodbye, give her instructions about certain church and personal documents, and admonished her to take care of their sons and his church. She began sobbing greatly and amidst her tears strongly rebuked him for such negative statements. He was a man of God and should have faith, and not be speaking of dying!

As she was speaking, Daniel saw two large angels (they were so large that he later wondered how they fit inside the ambulance – one was as big as the ambulance) who were completely white (even the pupils of their eyes). Daniel tried to speak to the angels, but one held his finger to his lips, motioning for his silence. The angels lifted him on either side, and Daniel realized that there were now two of himself. The angels were holding him under each arm of his spirit man (which was perfectly whole), while his broken body was lying below. Once they left the ambulance, Daniel became oblivious to the natural world.

When the ambulance arrived at Umezuruike Hospital with Daniel's body, it was now late at night (Friday, November 30th), and Daniel's doctor was not there. A member of the medical staff, however, examined his body and sadly told Nneka that her husband was dead and there was nothing that could be done. Nneka refused to believe the bad report. So, they drove to the Federal Medical Center in Owerri, but found no doctor there either. Finally, they drove to the Eunice Clinic, and there Daniel was confirmed to be dead by Doctor Jossy Anuebunwa. There was no breathing, no heartbeat or pulse, and Daniel's pupils were dilated and fixed. The doctor said that there was nothing he could do. A death certificate was issued at 11:30 P.M., November 30, 2001.

They then drove Daniel's corpse to his father's house in a nearby village, and naturally Daniel's father and other family members were heartbroken at the sight of Daniel's dead body, weeping profusely. Daniel's father instructed them to take his body to Ikeduru General Hospital Mortuary not far away. They arrived there around 1:00 A.M. on Saturday morning. The resident mortician, Mr. Darlington Manu, received the corpse and the family members departed.

The primitive Nigerian mortuary where Daniel's body was taken had no cold storage facilities, and so the mortician injected embalming chemicals into Daniel's fingers and into his feet. He then prepared to fully embalm Daniel's body by cutting Daniel's inner thigh in order to insert a tube by which he could inject more embalming fluid. As he did this, he experienced a shock that pushed him away from the corpse. This did not surprise him, as he had experienced similar forces before and attributed them to occult powers. (Such things are widely practiced in Africa and highly respected by all African pastors whom I know. Africans never understand the scepticism of Americans regarding the reality of occult power.) After a second attempt and a second shock that somewhat paralyzed his right arm, he concluded that Daniel must have been a member of a powerful secret society. He assumed, however, that after some occult sacrifices and incantations the powers in the corpse would subside, and he could then complete his work. (This mortician, of course, was not a Christian, but converted after Daniel's resurrection.) So, he instructed an assistant to lay Daniel's body in the rear of the mortuary where many other corpses were already laid.

Around 2:00 A.M. Saturday morning, the mortician, who lived very close to the mortuary, was disturbed by songs of worship coming from inside his mortuary, which stopped as soon as he approached the mortuary doorway. This occurred twice. Upon searching for the music's source in his mortuary, he noticed some kind of light emanating from the face of Daniel's corpse. This completely unnerved him.

The mortician was so disturbed over what was happening that he located Daniel's father on Saturday morning to inform him of what had been happening and to request that he remove Daniel's corpse from his mortuary. Then, on Saturday night, while she was sleeping, Daniel's wife experienced a dream in which she saw the face of her husband, and he was asking her why they had left him in the mortuary. He stated that he was not dead and that she should take him to Onitsha where German evangelist Reinhard Bonnke was preaching. She determined to do so, even though her family thought she was out of her mind. Daniel had been dead for more than 28 hours.

The family finally yielded but purchased a casket and brought funeral clothing for the mortician to dress Daniel. Rigor mortis had fully set in by this time. An ambulance was hired on Sunday morning, December 2nd, and the casket that contained Daniel's body was taken to Grace of God Mission (a large church) in Onitsha, about one and half hours away, where evangelist Reinhard Bonnke was preaching at an afternoon church dedication service. They arrived at the church around 1:00 P.M.

The church grounds were being protected by swarms of federal, state and local security guards for the sake of Reinhard Bonnke. And the security guards would not allow the casket to be brought onto church grounds, thinking it might actually contain explosives. Daniel's wife loudly pleaded with them and opened the casket to show them her dead husband, which resulted in their mocking and even flogging her because of her persistence to gain entrance. She caused such a disturbance that the senior pastor was notified, and his son instructed that Daniel's wife be permitted to bring his body to the church without the casket, and that it be placed in the basement. Daniel's body was laid there on two tables pushed together in a Sunday School room.

Some believers gathered around Daniel's body and prayed while Reinhard Bonnke, who knew nothing of the dead body in the basement, preached and prayed. Eventually, it was noticed that Daniel's corpse twitched, and then irregular breathing started. The attendant believers began praying fervently, and because his body was stiff and cold, they began massaging his neck, arms and legs. When those in the sanctuary got word that a dead man below was coming back to life, the basement room was soon jammed with people. Suddenly Daniel sneezed and arose with a jump. It was somewhere between 3:50 and 5:15 PM on Sunday afternoon. Daniel had died Friday night around 10:00 PM. He slowly became fully coherent over the next few hours.

End Notes:
i.   http://www.theheavenandhell.net/hell/daniel-ekechukwu/ see also "To Hell and Back" by Bisi Daniels – Busy Creations Oniru, Lagos, Nigeria

CHAPTER NINE

Alternative views of heaven and hell

"The concept of the universe as a divine kingdom over which God as King rules sovereignly is a familiar theme in the Scriptures" (1 Chronicles 29:11-12).

The only significance of life consists in helping to establish the kingdom of God. Leo Tolstoy

Introduction

Countless books have been written to expound the precise meaning of the kingdom in the Scriptures. In the Hebrew calendar beginning on 15th day of Shvat until and including 30th day of Shvat (i) the theme is 'Building the Kingdom" and then 'Signs of the Kingdom'. I have never seen anything similar in the Common Lectionary. It is a subject of immense importance to the Jewish believer and it should also be for the Gentile Church too.

Among conservative evangelical scholars there is general agreement that God is sovereign over the universe. However, challenging this sovereignty is the kingdom of evil, ruled over by Satan (Matthew 12:26). There are also earthly kingdoms over which God has allowed men to rule (Daniel 4:17). It was this kingdom that Satan offered to Jesus during the testing in the wilderness (Matthew 4:8-11).

A spiritual rule of God also exists in the hearts and lives of those who put their trust in Jesus Christ. The precise character of the kingdom and its place in the unfolding of the divine plan of God remains controversial and confusing to us, but not to God, as the previous chapters have shown. 'Heaven is a place, not just a state of mind' **(ii)** Two passages in Acts of the Apostles confirm this. *"Men of Galilee," they said, "why do you stand here looking into the sky? This same Jesus, who has been taken from you into heaven, will come back in the same way you have seen him go into heaven."* (Acts 1:11) and *"But Stephen, full of the Holy Spirit, looked up to heaven and saw the glory of God, and Jesus standing at the right hand of God. "Look," he said, "I see heaven open and the Son of Man standing at the right hand of God."* (Acts 7:55-56)

In Chapter Six we looked at God's timeline for Heaven and Hell. There are four applications of the kingdom to the Millennium that I have described there, and two of these, Historic Premillennialism and Amillennialism have quite different concepts of the kingdom. They both raise concerns about the earthly phase of the divine kingdom. The diagram of the Historic Premillennial position clearly shows that after the Second Coming there will be a thousand-year millennium period during which, Jesus reigns from Jerusalem, compared to the Amillennial concept of the kingdom of God as having its primary earthly fulfilment in the church age. There are several influential books on this **(iii)**. In neither position is there a rapture event and in both positions the saints are on earth during the Tribulation period, contrary to the promise of God in Scripture to protect the Church from the Tribulation. There are several reasons stated in Scripture why the Rapture will take the Church to be with Jesus before the Tribulation period begins. These are (for more details see God's Glorious promise **(iv)**).

(i)   In the Bible we see that God never judges the righteous with the wicked (Nahum 1 v. 2-3). Consider the examples of Noah and his family, Lot and his family re Sodom and Gomorrah. Noah's Ark represents Christ and believers are in Christ, who is our eternal refuge.

(ii)   Writing to Christians in Thessalonica Paul says in 1 Thessalonians 5 v. 9 'God did not appoint us to suffer wrath . . .' (i.e. Judgement). The purpose of the Tribulation is God's judgement on all unbelievers including unbelieving Israel. Praise God as we shall see in later chapters Israel finally accepts Jesus as their Messiah during the Tribulation. There is no reason for believers to go through the Tribulation for by believing on Jesus and accepting His offer of forgiveness for all our sins through the shedding of His blood on the Cross, He has taken the judgement for our sins on Himself.

(iii)   The Church is not mentioned again in the Bible after Revelation 3 v. 22. Why is this? Because the Church is in heaven as Revelation Chapters 4 and 5 indicate and this is before the Tribulation starts in Revelation Chapter 6. The 24 elders are representative of the 12 Tribes of Israel thus the Old Testament saints and the 12 apostles representing the New Testament saints being the Church

(iv)   In 2 Thessalonians 2 v. 1-8 it indicates that the antichrist cannot emerge and come to power until after the Holy Spirit and the Church have been removed.

(v)   Bearing in mind that all the events in the Book of Revelation are in chronological order, in Revelation

19 the wedding of the Lamb occurs before Christ's Second Coming and the Battle of Armageddon.

(vi) When a country is set to go to war against another country, the first thing it does before battle commences is to withdraw its ambassador and people. We are Christ's ambassadors (2 Corinthians 5 v. 20) and the Tribulation is a time of God's judgemental warfare against the unrepentant wicked in the world, so it stands to reason that God's people will be withdrawn from the earth before His judgements begin.

(vii). In Revelation 3 v. 10 Jesus states to the Christians in Sardis and all Christians that, '. . . I will keep you from the hour of trial that is going to come upon the whole world to test those who live on the earth.' The word 'from' is literally translated 'out of' while the word 'trial' affecting the whole world is a reference to the Tribulation. This is the blessed hope Paul talks about in Titus 2 v. 13.

When Jesus talks to His disciples in John 14 v. 2-3 I believe He is referring to the Rapture of the Church when He says, 'In my Father's house are many rooms; if it were not so, I would have told you. And if I go and prepare a place for you, I will come back and take you to be with me . . .' In this way, I believe that we could define the Rapture event as being 'from kingdom to kingdom.

1 Thessalonians 4 v. 13-18 is the main passage of scripture regarding the Rapture of the Church. One of the strongest arguments in favour of a pre-tribulation rapture is found in 1 Thessalonians 5 v. 11 because I think it would be hard for Christians to encourage one another if they were due to go through the Tribulation.

This Thessalonian passage of scripture is not referring to the Second Coming of Jesus, firstly, as it clearly says in v. 17 that we are going to meet the Lord in the air and, secondly, in Zechariah Ch 14 v. 4 it says that Jesus is going to stand on the Mount of Olives at His Second Coming and then the battle of Armageddon will immediately take place (Revelation 19 v. 19-21). Those who would deny the Rapture event clearly ignore the Biblical facts. For example:

1 Thessalonians 4 vv. 13-18 is the main passage of Scripture regarding the Rapture of the Church. One of the strongest arguments in favour of a pre-tribulation rapture is found in 1 Thessalonians 5 v. 11 because I think it would be hard for Christians to encourage one another if they were due to go through the Tribulation. 1 Thessalonians 4:17 is not referring to the Second Coming of Jesus as it clearly says that we are going to meet the Lord in the air.

In Zechariah chapter 14 v. 4 it says that Jesus is going to stand on the Mount of Olives at His Second Coming and then the battle of Armageddon will immediately take place (Revelation 19 vv. 19-21).

Views of the kingdom of heaven that do not include the Rapture event are the position that most liberal theologians, as well as conservative amillennialists, take. Christians holding this liberal view believe the kingdom of heaven to be equivalent to the concept of the kingdom of God that is fulfilled in the spiritual rule of God in the hearts of those who put their trust in Christ. In both cases this is said to happen at the second coming of Christ, although it is never explained how Christians who are 'born-again' (John 3:1-8) and filled with the Spirit (Ephesians 5:18), call Him 'Father' (Romans 8:15-16) and have the assurance that they are in the kingdom of God now are not living under the lordship of Christ!

Numerous scholars have pointed out variations to the Amillennial position just outlined as further alternative views of Heaven. For example, they cite the theory of Albert Ritschl, who regarded the kingdom as the unification of the human race, prompted by universal love. Others consider the kingdom as future, illustrated in the view of Albert Schweitzer, who anticipated a future intrusion of God into history. Apparently, Neo-orthodox theologians also contemplate a future time when the social order will be brought to perfection, when human history is caught up in divine history. **(v)**

Further alternative views can be found within premillennialism because of different interpretation of the same Scripture. There is no unity in the Premillennialist position between the present form of the kingdom and the future millennial form of the kingdom as proposed by Post Millennialists. I do not agree with these views because they do not correctly interpret the kingdom of God/heaven passages and because eschatologically they arrive at the wrong meaning. For example, in Matthew the seven parables of the kingdom of heaven (Chapter 13) are set in the context of the future kingdom which is for believing Israel rather than the equivalent Markan parables (4:1-29) that relate to the present kingdom of God in which Christ is Servant and not King. Israel, to whom these parables are addressed do not believe and do not understand, as is the case today with unbelieving gentiles. Thus, they cannot yet be citizens of the kingdom and faithful to God's rule, but they can hear the word of truth about what it will be and hear about the servant heart of Christ who died for the forgiveness of their sins. There is, therefore, for the unbeliever, a difference between the present form of the kingdom and the eternal kingdom, namely salvation.

The Kingdom of heaven and of God

There is a passage in Matthew 11:12 that always attracted me to what I have seen as the reality of kingdom living in these days. It is 'strong' men and women who lay hold of the kingdom and whose witness is therefore powerful and persuasive. Don Carson in his book on the Beatitudes **(vi)** sees this in the context of Jesus fulfilling the prophetic law and the prophets. He writes "The entire Old Testament has a prophetic function; and Jesus came to fulfil the Old Testament". He is saying that the Kingdom of Heaven which is forcefully advancing against the violence of opposers, is the fulfilment of Old Testament prophecy. To a generation that was in unbelief this was unacceptable and so they rejected both the Kingdom and its King (Matthew 11:20-24) **(vii).**

When preachers are being trained in theological college, they will often be taught that two different expressions are used to describe the Kingdom of Heaven. In meaning, 'kingdom of heaven' we are taught, is identical to 'kingdom of God'. They cite Matthew 19:23-30 and Mark 10:23-31 as examples to justify this assertion. I take this view and I simply believe that the kingdom of heaven and the kingdom of God are the same.

In addition, we should also understand that firstly the idea of 'kingdom' in both Old and New Testaments is primarily dynamic rather than spatial, in other words it is about the reign of God rather than just the place of His reign. Secondly, authority to rule this kingdom has been given to Jesus (Matthew 28:18) who mediates God's authority until God has put all His enemies under His feet (1 Corinthians 15:25). It is interesting to note that in His sermon on the Mount, Jesus seems to limit the universality of the Kingdom of Heaven, by setting conditions upon those who may enter it. In Matthew's gospel therefore, it is:

(i)   "The poor in spirit" (5:3),

(ii)   "the obedient" (7:21),

(iii)   "the righteous" (5:20)

(iv)   and in John's gospel it is those who "are born again by the Spirit" (3:3-8) who can enter the Kingdom of (heaven).

This must indicate that whilst the Kingdom of God and of heaven whilst universal, is for all believers. Thus, the Kingdom of Heaven is about a focus on salvation and therefor life in all its fullness (John 10:10) over which God's sovereignty applies eternally.

How we enter the kingdom is uniquely important. For example, in Mark's gospel it is better to enter life crippled than to have two feet and be thrown into hell (Mark 9:45) or to pluck out your eye if it causes you to sin than have two eyes and be thrown into hell (Mark 9:47). God's plan is that we enter life and the kingdom of heaven at the same time because we cannot have one without the other! (see Matthew 5:3,10; 7:21 and 7:31)

The Kingdom of God is described by Jesus in His parable of the sower (Matthew 13:24-29; 36-43) in which the sower (The Lord) finds that weeds (Satan's deceptions, false teaching and activity) have sprouted up alongside wheat (The true children of the kingdom) to counterfeit, confuse and separate them from God. This illustrates that the present kingdom embraces both men with life and men without life (i.e. both saved and unsaved). The separation comes at the Rapture. The kingdom of heaven will come at harvest time (The Second Coming) at which time only by the wheat (believers) which, metaphorically speaking, is gathered into the master's barn/heaven (Matthew 13:30). The New Testament speaks of God's kingdom now for those who have been saved and have life in all its fullness (John 10:10) but points to the fact that the kingdom will only be inherited in the future at Jesus second coming. We can summarise this as follows:

a) All believers have eternal life

b) At the rapture all believers will have their new bodies (See Gods Glorious Promise)

c) Believers will be with the Lord for eternity after the Final Judgement and the coming of the New Heaven and Earth

d) Believers have a Spirit life now but a spatial life after the Second Coming

Jesus tells a parable of the ten minas to illustrate this truth in Luke 19:11-27. The Jews who rejected Jesus also rejected His kingdom, but the parable is intended to show that the kingdom will come with visible manifestation at the Second Coming. In the parable the man of noble birth represents Jesus who will receive for himself a kingdom to be established at His second coming. The ten servants represent the same groups as the ten virgins of Matthew 25:1-13 in which Israel at the end of the Tribulation will comprise the believing remnant (five wise virgins) who will enter the Messianic kingdom and the unbelieving Jews (five foolish virgins) who will be excluded from the Messianic kingdom. The timing of the coming of the kingdom is dealt with in Luke 17:20-37. Here Luke makes clear that the kingdom will not come until after Jesus suffering and rejection (v25) and then Judgement (vv26-37). Verse 27 deals with the terrible reality of Armageddon (see Revelation 16:14 and 19:17). The Timeline in Appendix A shows the Battle of Armageddon at the end of the Tribulation and at the Second Coming of the Lord.

Eternal life although experienced now will only be consummated after the Final Judgement and the arrival of "the New Heaven and a New Earth" (Isaiah 65:17; 66:22; 2 Peter 3:13 and Revelation 21:1).

We can illustrate this by the following diagram: **(vi)**

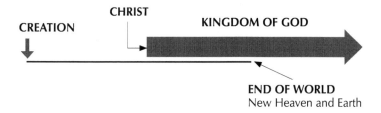

CHRIST

CREATION

KINGDOM OF GOD

END OF WORLD
New Heaven and Earth

It is said by scholars, like Wayne Grudem, **(viii)** that much of the confusion in the argument concerning the meaning of the kingdom of heaven and kingdom of God has arisen, from the mistaken judgment that the distinction between the kingdom of heaven and the kingdom of God is a dispensational one. In other words, that these two distinct kingdoms were granted by God at different times, one now and the other a future kingdom. The facts, Grudem argues, are to the contrary, as it is purely an exegetical problem, that is the correct interpretation of scripture. In a word, the issue is whether the present form of the kingdom, whether it be kingdom of God or kingdom of heaven, is the predicted millennial form. Amillennialists tend to affirm that it is. Premillennialists look for a future fulfilment at the Second Coming of Christ and after the Final Judgement. The great theme in Matthews Gospel chapters 5,6 & 7 is the "Kingdom of Heaven". Ignoring scholarly arguments for the moment, we can say that "Kingdom of Heaven" is the expression that Matthew uses for "The Kingdom of God". He does this because, like many Jews of his day, Matthew did not want to misuse the holy name of God. I have to say that my belief is that the kingdom of God and heaven mean the same thing.

True features of the Kingdom of God and the Kingdom of Heaven

A careful study of Scripture will reveal the following features of both:

- both are at hand;
- both are entered only by the righteous
- both include saved men;
- both grow rapidly;
- both are difficult to enter;
- both have 'leaven', symbolic of bad doctrine, externalism, unbelief, and worldliness; There will be the leaven of sin in the Millennium but not of wrong teaching. This

is because Jesus will rule with a rod of iron during the Millennium and there will be no false teaching.

- both contain Gentiles.

Because the two expressions, in my view, are one and the same and the fact that *heaven* is sometimes used as an equivalent for God, many scholars have taken the position that the terms are identical or at least are used as synonyms.

Entry to the Kingdom of Heaven

One false view of the Kingdom of Heaven concerns the question about who can enter it. For example, some scholars who distinguish the kingdom of heaven from the kingdom of God do so on the principle that the kingdom of heaven seems to include not only those who are saved, but some unsaved men who profess salvation. On the other hand, many more evangelical scholars would argue that the kingdom of God when used of a spiritual kingdom, includes only saved men and elect angels, which is my position too. The New Testament makes this clear. As Nicodemus met Jesus at night to ask about entry to the Kingdom, Jesus turns the focus onto the Kingdom of God and makes clear that one cannot enter the kingdom of God without being born again or born from above (John 3:3- 8). This is supported by the Apostle Paul in his letter to the Roman, where he says, "for the kingdom of God is not a matter of eating and drinking, but of righteousness, peace and joy in the Holy Spirit" (Romans 14:17).

Jesus taught in the Sermon on the Mount (Matthew 8:10-12) that many would come from all over the world and enter His Kingdom. Whereas those unbelieving Jews and all unbelievers, 'the subjects of the kingdom' he said, would be thrown outside, into the darkness, where there would be weeping and gnashing of teeth. Whilst the Jews were privileged to be inheritors of the Old Testament revelation, their rejection of Jesus as Messiah, precluded them for entry into that Kingdom of God where there is life. Jesus also warned that many who would be expected to enter the Kingdom would be excluded.

In 1 Corinthians 15:50 additional confirmation is given in the statement, "Flesh and blood cannot inherit the kingdom of God." The context goes on to speak of the translation and the resurrection of the righteous. This again could not refer to those who are merely professing faith, but only to those genuinely saved. As the context of this text is still the resurrection body, no physical body which is contaminated by the old sin nature can enter the heaven eternal heaven, only the resurrected body which has no sin. (see Chapter One)

When we think of the kingdom of heaven and who can enter it, as previously discussed, we find a different picture. Perhaps this picture is more about the Church and Christians generally until the Judgement of believers works on the one hand or the Final Judgement on the other, depending upon the true nature of the saved person. In Matthew 13:24-30 and interpreted in verses 36-43, Jesus is talking about the Kingdom of Heaven using the analogy of the farmer sowing seed in the field which produces both wheat and tares, with the separation coming only at the time of harvest. This is a picture of profession, as the tares look like the wheat, but their true character will be revealed at the final judgment. The same basic concept is also brought out in the parable of the dragnet in Matthew 13:47-52; where the net, which is compared to the kingdom of heaven, gathers of every kind. Those thus gathered are not separated until the final judgment or the consummation of this age.

Entry into the Kingdom of God is not easy and is not by what evangelicals call 'works', although the daily response to Jesus saving grace is something that we work at. For example, Jesus talks about a rich man and a needle to illustrate this point. In both Matthew 19:24 and Mark 10:17-23 he says: "It is easier for a camel to go through the eye of a needle than for a rich man to enter the kingdom of God" and," How hard it is for the rich to enter the Kingdom of God". The fact that

Matthew goes out of his way to use the expression "kingdom of God" here in contrast to his normal expression "kingdom of heaven" is supported by the statement which clearly refers to the sphere of salvation rather than to the sphere of profession. The final reference in Matthew to the kingdom of God is found in Matthew 21:28-32 (the parable of the Two Sons), where Jesus said: "I tell you the truth I say unto you, that the publicans and the harlots go into the kingdom of God before you" (ASV). Although the religious rulers of the Jews made a profession of following God which could be said to be in the widest sphere of profession, (Unger's P485 refers to this as 'the empty externalist') Christ here again is talking of the sphere of reality or of salvation, and so Matthew's Gospel uses the expression "the kingdom of God" in this instance.

In these instances where the context clearly refers to the sphere of salvation, it is most significant that Matthew goes out of his way to use the expression "kingdom of God." If he had not done so and had substituted the expression "kingdom of heaven," it would of course be most difficult to maintain that the kingdom of heaven is the sphere of profession **(ix)**.

End Notes:

i. **In Time with God, daily Devotional Bible Readings in accordance with the Biblical Hebrew Calendar**: R K Bamber – In Time with God Publications

ii. **Systematic Theology, Ch 57 outline A2** – Wayne Grudem

iii. Examples of these include Richard Swinburne's "A Theodicy of heaven and hell" In the Existence and Nature of God" edited by Alfred J Freddoso (Notre Dame Press 1983) and Thomas Talbott "A case for Christian Universalism" In Universal Salvation: the Current Debate, edited by Robin Parry and Chris Partridge, Paternoster 2003

iv. **God's Glorious Promise**: Baguley & French – New Wine Press
v.   Examples taken from "The Kingdom of Heaven" contributed by www.Walvoord.com are *The Kingdom of God* by John Bright. J. Dwight Pentecost's *Things to Come*; *The Greatness of the Kingdom*, by Alva McClain; and Dr John F Walvoord's *The Millennial Kingdom*.
vi. **The Sermon on the Mount**: D A Carson – Baker Book House
vii. **The Sermon on the Mount** p14: D A Carson – Baker Book House
viii. **Systematic Theology**: Wayne Grudem: Zondervan
ix. Taken from "The Kingdom of Heaven" contributed by www.Walvoord.com are *The Kingdom of God* by John Bright. J. Dwight Pentecost's *Things to Come*; *The Greatness of the Kingdom*, by Alva McClain; and Dr John F Walvoord's *The Millennial Kingdom*.

APPENDIX A

God's timeline for heaven and hell

GOD'S TIME LINE FOR HEAVEN AND HELL

Pentecost

Pre-Millennium

Rapture

Second Coming

Saints with Christ
in heaven

With the Saints
to earth to reign with Him

New Heaven & Earth

Saints in heaven
with Jesus

CHURCH AGE
Heaven on
Earth

TRIBULATION
7 Years

3 ½ yrs

3 ½ yrs
Great Trib

MILLENNIUM
1000 years (Isaiah 9:6-7)
(Isaiah 11:6-9)
Satan bound for 1000 years
in abyss Revelation 20:1-3

GREAT WHITE
THRONE JUDGEMENT

Revelation 20:11-14

Satan loosed to be thrown into
Eternal lake of fire (Revelation 20:10)

Eternal hell in Lake of Fire

WW3

WW4

WW5

Russia invasion of Israel WW3

Ezekiel 38 & Revelation 6:3-4

Battle of Armageddon Rev 19:19-21

Battle of Gog & Magog Revelation 20:6-10

154

APPENDIX B

Blood showers (getting in)

One modern song that encapsulates the cost and truth of our Saviours death is **Nothing but the Blood** by **Matt Redman.** The Lyrics are as follows:

Your blood speaks a better word
Than all the empty claims I've heard upon this earth
Speaks righteousness for me
And stands in my defence
Jesus, it's Your blood
Your blood

Your blood speaks a better word
Than all the empty claims I've heard upon this earth
Speaks righteousness for me
And stands in my defence
Jesus, it's Your blood

What can wash away our sins?
What can make us whole again?
Nothing but the blood
Nothing but the blood of Jesus
What can wash us pure as snow
Welcomed as the friends of God?
Nothing but Your blood
Nothing but Your blood, King Jesus

Your cross testifies in grace
Tells of the Father's heart to make a way for us
Now boldly we approach
Not earthy confidence
It's only by Your blood

Chorus

It's Your blood, it's Your blood
Oh
It's Your blood, it's Your blood

One of the most exciting questions that we may be asked is "How may I be saved?" or "How can I know Jesus?". Evangelism enables this privilege not just with Anglo-Saxon British people but with those from other cultures, countries and faiths who live or work in the UK. The question is a deep one, because implicitly, it is asking another question "How may I enter Heaven? Or, as the Rich Young Ruler asked, *"How may I inherit Eternal Life?"* (Luke 18:18-30). Jesus' answer challenges the rich young ruler to re-evaluate his understanding of faith by selling everything he has and giving it to the poor. Jesus was not setting out a new doctrine of helping the financially poor but drawing attention to the true value of the Kingdom. Is it wealth or eternal life? Which one grips you more? As we cannot buy our way into heaven then logically money is of no importance to our salvation. If we cling on to a love of money, then our witness and walk of faith will be weakened and become subservient to money. The parable of the Rich Young Ruler is very challenging today to the many 'millionaires' and wealthy people now resident, or not, in the UK.

The Apostle Peter hammers home this central message about salvation when he wrote, *"For you know that it was not with perishable things such as silver or gold that you were redeemed from the empty way of life handed down to you from your ancestors, but with the precious blood of Christ, a lamb without blemish or defect."* (1 Peter 1:19)

Another chorus song "Only by blood may we enter" is a poignant reminder of this Biblical truth that salvation, new life and entry to the eternal kingdom are only through the shed blood of Jesus Christ and the new birth by the Holy Spirit. William Booth's Hymn "Send the Fire" with the great line "Your blood bought gifts today we claim" is another wonderful way of proclaiming the same truth. This blood covenant is uniquely God's, both as a sacrificial system of worship in the Old Testament and through the death and resurrection of Jesus recorded in the New Testament.

It may be somewhat reductionist to say, but for our purposes of this appendix we will reduce the teaching to three parts (each describing some aspect about the blood of Jesus): It is not an 'either or' but an 'all and'. The three aspects are

SAVED BY THE BLOOD
SEALED IN THE BLOOD
STRENGTHENED THROUGH THE BLOOD

There is a wonderful verse in the book of Revelation that sums it all up as follows:

They were singing him a new song with these words: "You are worthy to take the scroll and break its seals and open it; for you were slain, and your blood has bought people from every nation as gifts for God (Revelation 5:9)

SAVED BY THE BLOOD

As our OT reading revealed, Moses sprinkled the blood of the Covenant upon the elders and people as the young bulls were sacrificed. The blood from the bulls was poured into bowls, half was used for sprinkling on the people and the other to throw on the altar. The link with the New Covenant is in the blood: In

Leviticus we are told by Moses that *"for the life of a creature is in the blood, and I have given it to you to make atonement for yourselves on the altar; it is the blood that makes atonement for one's life."* (Leviticus 17:11)-

The Apostle John in his Revelation on Patmos witnessed the worship in heaven, and the declaration that what Jesus Christ did was to purchase salvation for us.

We are so used to taking a shower these days – in fact some people are devoted to it. Seeking cleanliness or psychologically washing away guilt – a laudable as that is, it doesn't and can't do what God does. Would we queue to have a blood shower? That's the one that we need. No water charges – in fact, it's free and undeserved. The mercy of God and the grace of the Lord Jesus – can we jump under the shower? Every day? and wash inside out. Water is skin deep; the blood is heart and soul deep! In Hebrews 9:11-20 (NIV) we read about The Blood of Christ, *"But when Christ came as high priest of the good things that are now already here, he went through the greater and more perfect tabernacle that is not made with human hands, that is to say, is not a part of this creation. He did not enter by means of the blood of goats and calves; but he entered the Most Holy Place once for all by his own blood, thus obtaining eternal redemption. The blood of goats and bulls and the ashes of a heifer sprinkled on those who are ceremonially unclean sanctify them so that they are outwardly clean. How much more, then, will the blood of Christ, who through the eternal Spirit offered himself unblemished to God, cleanse our consciences from acts that lead to death, so that we may serve the living God! For this reason, Christ is the mediator of a new covenant, that those who are called may receive the promised eternal inheritance—now that he has died as a ransom to set them free from the sins committed under the first covenant.*

SEALED IN THE BLOOD

So, when we take that blood shower, something else supernatural happens . . . the new person is sealed in with the righteousness of Jesus. Paul writing to the Jews and Gentile believers in Rome (Romans 3:24-26 NIV) says

> and all are justified freely by his grace through the redemption that came by Christ Jesus. God presented Christ as a sacrifice of atonement, through the shedding of his blood – to be received by faith. He did this to demonstrate his righteousness, because in his forbearance he had left the sins committed beforehand unpunished – he did it to demonstrate his righteousness at the present time, so as to be just and the one who justifies those who have faith in Jesus.

Also, integrity and identity are sealed in the blood. (Romans 10:10-11)

STRENGTHENED THROUGH THE BLOOD

Hebrews 11:33-35 New International Version (NIV) says:

> "who through faith conquered kingdoms, administered justice, and gained what was promised; who shut the mouths of lions, quenched the fury of the flames, and escaped the edge of the sword; whose weakness was turned to strength; and who became powerful in battle and routed foreign armies. Women received back their dead, raised to life again. There were others who were tortured, refusing to be released so that they might gain an even better resurrection".

We are prepared for service, our identity sealed and we are strengthened by the blood of Jesus for every good work (Hebrews 13:20-21) and I finish with these verses from the letter of Jude 20-21:-

Benediction and Final Greetings

Now may the God of peace, who through the blood of the eternal covenant brought back from the dead our Lord Jesus, that great Shepherd of the sheep, equip you with everything good for doing his will, and may he work in us what is pleasing to him, through Jesus Christ, to whom be glory for ever and ever. **Amen**

APPENDIX C

Money and camels
(problems getting in)

Towards the end of Matthew's Gospel, we move from Jesus's active ministry in Galilee to Jesus teaching about the Kingdom. In Capernaum, he answers the tax collector's question about Temple tax (Matthew 17:24-27). The question was very much about tax paid to the Temple authorities', but Jesus answered it, in the Rabbinic style by asking a *question "From whom do kings of the earth collect duty and taxes – from their own sons or others?"* (v25), The annual temple tax required every male of over 20 years in age to pay the tax of half a shekel or two drachma's (approximately two days wages) (see Exodus 30:13; 2 Chronicles 24:9 & Nehemiah 10:32) and was used for the upkeep of the Temple. Peter's answer to Jesus' question and Jesus response make it clear that just as the sons of the temple leaders were exempt then so are the sons of God (born-again believers) from the cost of the upkeep of God's temple of believers because the cost has already been paid by Jesus. Entry is by faith and not by 'good works' or taxes.

Chapter eighteen records Jesus teaching about the Kingdom before Jesus moved to Judea and Perea (chapter nineteen) where further teaching on children and divorce took place. We then come to the issue of eternal life and entry into salvation and eternal life. This takes the form of an encounter between Jesus and a Rich Young Ruler (recorded by both Mark and Luke). The question on the heart of the young ruler was a very contemporary one *"What good thing must I do to get eternal life?"* This question raises a number of important points. Firstly, there is the question of **Righteousness** – namely can it be bought or earned or even demanded, all of which a wealthy person used to using his power and position might think can be used. Jesus has to correct this wrong understanding before answering the question asked of him. The second point is that of **Eternal life**. It is interesting that this is the first time in Matthew's gospel that the term is used. It is true that John uses it much more frequently whereas the Gospels of Mark and Luke treat the terms "Kingdom of heaven/eternal life synonymously (as described in earlier chapters). The third point concerns that of **Goodness.** The rich young ruler must learn that goodness is not a reward or merit for keeping the commandments. Only God is good and only 'sonship' and the indwelling of the Holy Spirit brings forth 'goodness' as a fruit of the Spirit (Galatians 5:19-22).

Jesus commend to the rich young ruler must have shaken him and shifted his wrong beliefs as well as challenging him to a radical new way of thinking and living, Jesus told him *"if you want to enter life, obey the commandments"* (v17) Jesus said this, not to establish merit, but to demonstrate true faith because salvation is if gift of God's grace only received by faith in the saving work of Christ upon the cross (Ephesians 2:8). No wonder the rich young man went away sad, because his wealth could not save him. Even the disciples were astonished at this because Jesus told them "Then Jesus said to his disciples, *"Truly I tell you, it is hard for someone who is rich to enter the kingdom of heaven. Again, I tell you, it is easier for a camel to go through the eye of a needle than for someone who is rich to enter the kingdom of God." When the disciples heard this, they were greatly astonished and asked, "Who then can be saved?"* This astonished the disciples because they knew that the camel was the largest animal found in Israel. The contrast between the largest animal and the smallest opening was intended to show how hard it is for man to enter into eternal life, other than by faith in the death and resurrection of Jesus Christ. (see also Mark 10:24-25)

In another passage in Matthew's gospel we read again of this problem for the rich, religious and unbelievers to enter into the kingdom of heaven – eternal life – the resurrection of the body – and the security of the believer. The Berean study Bible translates Matthew 23:24 as follows:

"Woe to you, scribes and Pharisees, you hypocrites! You pay tithes of mint, dill, and cumin, but you have disregarded the weightier matters of the law: justice, mercy, and faithfulness. You should have practiced the latter, without neglecting the former. You blind guides! You strain out a gnat but swallow a camel. Woe to you, scribes and Pharisees, you hypocrites! You clean the outside of the cup and dish, but inside they are full of greed and self-indulgence . . . The strict Pharisees would carefully strain their drinking water through a cloth to be sure that they did not swallow a gnat, the smallest of unclean animals, but figuratively they would swallow a camel!

As we consider 'which way we are heading, heaven or hell, this teaching by Jesus given in the context of His Kingdom, helps us to see the signposts to faith and eternal life and to avoid the pitfalls of unbelief, wealth, religious spirits, and unrighteousness given through these texts. Thanks be to God!

APPENDIX D

Rich and poor

The destination of those who do not attain to God's righteousness by accepting Jesus Christ as the Word and the Saviour is what the Bible calls the second death (Revelation 20:14-15)

The Bible teaches us clearly that there is a divide between the believer and the unbeliever. Without Jesus and apart from Him the unbeliever has no way of overcoming the problem of sin and judgement.

The Apostle Paul underscores this truth in his letter to the Romans chapter 6 verse 23 in which he says, *"For the wages of sin is death, but the gift of God is eternal life in Christ Jesus our Lord"*. This sets the scene for Jesus teaching about the Rich man and Lazarus.

The Rich Man and Lazarus (LUKE 16:19-31)

We should not think that this is a parable. It is instead an actual historical illustration used by Jesus to show the sneering and pompous Pharisees that their wealth and outward form of righteousness would not save them and that it was, in fact, a fallacy. This story about the rich man and Lazarus gives us some important details about death. Both characters in the story died before Jesus died on the cross and are Old Testament figures.

In the story the rich man's great wealth was not evidence, as the Pharisees would think, of divine favour for despite his wealth he went to hell because he was not a believer. On the other hand, Lazarus, a penniless beggar and a believer who lived in abject poverty, went to Abraham's bosom. Between the rich man and Lazarus was an impassable gulf separating the lost from the saved. In using this illustration Jesus opens a curtain to life after death revealing the place of departed souls, both saved and unsaved between death and resurrection. (See Unger's Bible Handbook). The NIV text reads:

"There was a rich man who was dressed in purple and fine linen and lived in luxury every day. At his gate was laid a beggar named Lazarus, covered with sores and longing to eat what fell from the rich man's table. Even the dogs came and licked his sores.

"The time came when the beggar died, and the angels carried him to Abraham's side. The rich man also died and was buried. In Hades, where he was in torment, he looked up and saw Abraham far away, with Lazarus by his side. So, he called to him, 'Father Abraham, have pity on me and send Lazarus to dip the tip of his finger in water and cool my tongue, because I am in agony in this fire.'

"But Abraham replied, 'Son, remember that in your lifetime you received your good things, while Lazarus received bad things, but now he is comforted here, and you are in agony. And besides all this, between us and you a great chasm has been set in place, so that those who want to go from here to you cannot, nor can anyone cross over from there to us.' "He answered, 'Then I beg you, father, send Lazarus to my family, for I have five brothers. Let him warn them, so that they will not also come to this place of torment.'

"Abraham replied, 'They have Moses and the Prophets; let them listen to them.'
"'No, father Abraham,' he said, 'but if someone from the dead goes to them, they will repent.' "He said to him, 'If they do not listen to Moses and the Prophets, they will not be convinced even if someone rises from the dead.'"

So, to the story of the rich man and Lazarus. This, as has already been noted, reveals the startling difference between heaven and hell. The one is paradise, a place of comfort and glory and the other a place of suffering, agony and torment. Jesus outlines the gulf between the two places (v26). The parable offers the stark consequence of unbelief. Another critical understanding concerns that of the difference between the death of the body and the awareness of the soul after death. Both men were asleep in their bodies (dead) but awake in their souls and able to feel, reason, to see and hear and communicate.

The Rich man neither believed nor understood the Law and the Prophets, even though he had the Law of Moses to help him, he lived in luxury and perhaps was idolatrous like the Israel's sister 'Sodom' and younger sister 'Samaria' (Jeremiah 3:6-11) was guilty of unfaithfulness and sin (see Ezekiel 16:49). As the rich man spoke to Abraham he began to think of others. He mentions his five brothers and suddenly realises that they are unbelievers too and will also end up in hell (v28). Abraham rebuked him because in his life time he had received many good things but never gave thanks for them or shared them (v25).

The poor man was a 'son of Abraham' through birth and faith. In the Talmud both Paradise and 'Abraham's bosom' are mentioned. Traditionally Abraham's bosom is home to the righteous because Abraham's faith was counted to him as righteous by God, Abraham's side is regarded as the place of blessedness to which the righteous dead go to await the resurrection. The poor man was a beggar and possibly was crippled like the lame man who begged outside the temple gate (Acts 3:2). He ate the crumbs from the rich man's table – a direct contrast with the faith of the Syrophoenician woman in Matthew 15:27 who recognised Jesus and the prodigal son in Luke 15:16 who ate pig swill.

Hell (or Hades Gk) is the place to which the wicked dead go to await final judgement. There is a huge chasm or gulf between the two and no way back from hell.

Jesus speaks of his own resurrection but makes the point that if someone has not believed in the OT (Law and prophets) then their mind is closed and even a resurrection would not change them (v31). The Pharisees are warned, but the message is also for unbelievers today who boast about their status, power and wealth or their intellectual ability and try to lord it over others without any care for them, ruling elite take note, EU leaders listen before it is too late. The chasm can be bridged before death by faith in the Lord Jesus to save and by repenting and turning to Him.

Finally, we must not dismiss this story simply as one to satisfy a curiosity about life after death. We are challenged to take note of the seriousness of <u>life before death</u>, because the choices that are made now determine our eternal joy or pain, whether we are rich or poor. This story underpins the importance of salvation to eternal life.

ABOUT THE AUTHOR

Andrew Baguley retired in 2009 after serving as Superintendent Methodist Minister in the UK Methodist Church. He has been involved with Church renewal and revival for over 20 years and, until recently, had pastoral charge of a small rural congregation in Hambledon, Hampshire. His heart is for sharing the gospel and ministering in the power of the Holy Spirit. He has seen many wonderful healings, some miracles and many become new Christians.

He has ministered at the Methodist International Prayer Conferences, the UMC Methodist International Prayer Conference, the UMC Aldersgate Conference, and in the Czech Republic, Slovakia, Germany, Singapore and the USA. He spoke in the past at 'Easter People' and many conferences in the UK. He has taught on the gifts of the Spirit, Christian holiness, training a church ministry team and equipping of emerging leaders at both Christ for the Nations Bible College in the UK, The Czech

United Methodist Church and at Hambledon Bible School, Hampshire UK.

Andrew has written six other books, Interceding for Revival, God's Glorious Promise (with Rev Roger French), Islam – Threat or Truth? Israel, A Sign and a Wonder, "Shaken", all published by New Wine Press and lastly "Where are we Heading? Heaven only Knows!" published by Lighthouse Publications. He is married to Joan and lives in Devon England. He has two daughters Julianne and Felicity and step daughters, Samantha and Sabrina, and is kept young by nine grandchildren and the occasional successes of Yorkshire County Cricket Club!

ACKNOWLEDGEMENTS

I wish to acknowledge the encouragement of many friends and colleagues as always in writing what will be seen by many as a controversial book. Thanks go to Rev Roger French and Danny Stupple, Jill Royston, Tony Stone, Dennis Greenidge, Tim Pearson and my family, especially Julianne & Ian who deal with the cover designs and artwork. Thanks also to Joan and my sister in law, Pauline. You are all encouragers. **God bless you**.

OTHER BOOKS BY THE AUTHOR

Interceding for Revival
God's Glorious Promise
Israel – A Sign and a Wonder
Islam – Threat or Truth?
Shaken
Where Are We Heading? – Heaven only Knows!

For further details and to order please visit my web site
www.andrewbaguley.co.uk

Andrew Baguley
UK Preacher, Evangelist and Author

Andrew Baguley has written many books, including
Islam – threat or truth, *Israel – A sign and a wonder*,
and *God's glorious promise*

www.andrewbaguley.co.uk